T0013232

"I remember sitting in Pennington's class wl reading the Scriptures. I had been taught tc ized this was a more beautiful practice. Pc have naturally read with this approach. Let Pennington guide you to a better reading where knowing God will come to life not only in your mind but in your whole being."

> **Patrick Schreiner,** Associate Professor, Midwestern Baptist Theological Seminary; author, *The Visual Word*; *The Kingdom of God and the Glory of the Cross*; and *The Mission of the Triune God*

"In *Come and See*, Jonathan Pennington serves as a faithful guide on the road trip of Bible reading. The church is in need of integrative approaches to reading the Bible, approaches that emphasize information, doctrine, and transformation. That is what this book is all about. If you want to be a better student of the Bible, do not wait to grab a copy of *Come and See*."

> **J. T. English,** Lead Pastor, Storyline Church; author, *Deep Discipleship*; Cofounder, Training the Church and *Knowing Faith Podcast*

Come and See

Come and See

The Journey of Knowing God through Scripture

Jonathan Pennington

:: CROSSWAY®

WHEATON, ILLINOIS

Library of Congress Cataloging-in-Publication Data

Names: Pennington, Jonathan T., author.
Title: Come and see : the journey of knowing God through scripture / Jonathan T. Pennington.
Description: Wheaton, Illinois : Crossway, 2023. | Includes bibliographical references and index.
Identifiers: LCCN 2022015449 (print) | LCCN 2022015450 (ebook) | ISBN 9781433571282 (trade paperback) | ISBN 9781433571312 (pdf) | ISBN 9781433571299 (epub)
Subjects: LCSH: Bible—Hermeneutics. | Bible—Criticism, interpretation, etc. | Bible—Reading.
Classification: LCC BS476 .P45 2023 (print) | LCC BS476 (ebook) | DDC 220.6—dc23/eng/20221130
LC record available at https://lccn.loc.gov/2022015449
LC ebook record available at https://lccn.loc.gov/2022015450

On June 7, 2022, while I was finishing the edits on this book, we learned that my wife, Tracy, had a large brain tumor. Our family's life was changed overnight. This book is dedicated to the Pennington Fam Plus crew who have grown even closer together and who are united in trusting that God is doing a thousand good things in every situation.

Contents

Introduction

Starting Out: Road Trip!

Come and see what God has done:
    he is awesome in his deeds toward the children of man.

PSALM 66:5

Oh, taste and see that the LORD is good!
    Blessed is the man who takes refuge in him!

PSALM 34:8

"Come and see." . . . "You will see heaven
opened, and the angels of God ascending
and descending on the Son of Man."

JOHN 1:46, 51

If you have ever made a road trip down the center of Tennessee on Interstate 24 toward Chattanooga, you probably recall seeing sign after sign encouraging you to "See Ruby Falls." The invitation to come and see Ruby Falls is painted on countless barn roofs and highway billboards along the way. They never say more than that, adding to the intrigue. You have to google it to learn who or what Ruby Falls is. Or you can take the exit and see it for yourself.

Either way, you'll learn that Ruby Falls is a stunning waterfall 1,120 feet below the surface of Lookout Mountain. It was discovered in 1928 and named after the wife of one of the excavators. The ubiquitous "See Ruby Falls" signs are an invitation to come, to look, to experience something worth seeing. This is a natural response to beauty. When we encounter something beautiful and good, we will inevitably want to tell others about it. Children don't need to be taught to say, "Dad, Mom, look!"

The Gospel of John includes lots of invitations to look, to behold, to see things wonderful. John the Baptist tells his hearers, "Look!" when he sees Jesus walking by because Jesus is "the Lamb of God, who takes away the sin of the world!" (John 1:29 NIV; see 1:36).

When the first two disciples encountered Jesus, he invited them by saying, "Come and you will see" (1:39). So they began following him. When another potential disciple, Nathanael, was skeptical that anything good could come out of Nazareth, his friend Philip used the same words, "Come and see" (1:46), to invite him to meet Jesus. And when Nathanael finally did see Jesus face to face and believed in him, Jesus promised that he would see much more. "You will see heaven opened, and the angels of God ascending and descending on the Son of Man" (1:51).

When the apostle John was penning these words, he wasn't just producing a historical record. All of these invitations to see simultaneously serve as an invitation from John to his readers. This includes us. The opening chapter of John's Gospel is an invitation *for us* to come and see Jesus in the pages of Holy Scripture. More beautiful and more important than seeing Ruby Falls is following the signs in Scripture to come and see Jesus. This is because, according to John, in seeing we will come to believe, and in believing we will come to have life eternal (20:31).

This same invitation to come and see, to taste and delight in God, is found throughout the Bible. The goal of reading the Scriptures is not merely to gain knowledge *about* God or to learn certain beliefs and behaviors. The real aim in reading Scripture is *to see and know God himself.* This won't fully occur until the redemption of the world that is called the new creation and the beatific vision (the happiness that comes from seeing God fully). But along the way, we get glimpses of what is to come. This happens especially through reading and studying the Bible. On this side of the new creation, Scripture is crucial for discovering the meaningful and flourishing life that will last for eternity.

The Road Trip Experience

There is nothing like the anticipation and excitement that comes with a road trip. Perhaps you remember such adventures with friends in high school and college—a small group of comrades who share your love for the same music and same junk food throwing together a few dollars and hitting the road. Pure joy. You have some destination and semi-plan roughed out in your heads, but that's all. It's really about the adventure as much as it is the destination: the unexpected scary or funny things that happen, the jokes that naturally emerge, the split-second decision to take exit 32 to seek out "Kicking Ash BBQ" or "The World's Largest Rubber Band Ball." These are what make the memories and immortalize the road trip.

During a stint as a youth pastor many years ago, I took the high school kids on an 899-mile, two-day trip from our church in northern Illinois to our denomination's youth conference in

Fort Collins, Colorado. This trip required a bit more detailed organization than the spontaneous road trips of my youth. I was in charge of renting fifteen-passenger vans, coordinating adult drivers, obtaining insurance, requesting permission slips, and more. Nonetheless, it was a road trip, and it was a transformative experience for all involved. The relationships that were formed, the subculture that was created, and the memories that were born combined to make our youth group different than it was before. Through our long journey together, we came to know and love one another more. This prepared us to meet with God at the mountaintop experience that only a massive youth conference in the Rockies can provide.

The significance of the road trip itself—not just the conference—hit home when two years later I took a group to the next biannual conference but this time in Indianapolis. Anticipation and expectations were high, especially for those who had been with me on the Colorado trip. And the conference was good. However, because the expedition took less than five hours, something crucial was lost. The trip was relatively quick with just one food stop. Relationships, memories, and stories didn't have enough baking time. Instead of a full-course meal, it was an existential snack. I realized more fully that the road trip itself was indeed as important as the conference.

The journey matters. Life is not a math problem to merely solve. It is a long series of conscious and unconscious moments that we as humans can only experience sequentially, not knowing fully what is coming next. The variation of experiences between the familiar (sweetened and deepened by time) and the new (awaking us again by stimulating our curiosity) is what makes the journey of our lives meaningful. The classic road trip forges and melds together these experiences into something beautiful. New and spontaneous adventures with old and growing friends—it doesn't get much better than that. That's why we love the road trip.

A Journey with Three Friends

This book has an important subtitle: *The Journey of Knowing God through Scripture*. This provides us with the metaphor or image by which we are invited to come and see God. We are going to think about reading the Bible as a journey, as a road trip. Knowing God is not just a pill we can swallow or an app we can open. It is a journey of life experiences that are shaped and interpreted over time by Scripture. The more we understand God's words, the more we will be able to make sense of our complicated lives. This little book is meant as a guide, a map, to help you make sense of what Scripture is saying. It is an invitation to take a road trip, the most life-giving and life-changing road trip possible.

But a road trip wouldn't be a road trip without good friends. You can make a journey alone; good can come from such reflective time. But the best trips, the ones that shape us, are the ones where a small group of people—individuals with their own quirks, strengths, and weaknesses—join together on the adventure.

For this road trip journey, we're joining up with a set of three great friends: Ingrid, Tom, and Taylor. These three friends are different in gender, background, interests, and passions, but they share a bond that is deeper than these limited elements of who they are. And this trip, taken together, is going to make them better people as they journey jointly and learn from one another.

Let's imagine this is a long trip, one where the friends need to share the driving. As the rules of the road trip go, the driver gets to choose the music and the podcasts to listen to. Ingrid, Tom, and

Taylor will each take a turn behind the wheel, and each will set the tone for his or her leg of the journey.

You may have already surmised what I'm doing with these images. These three friends each represent a certain mode of reading, a particular timbre, a kind of approach that is distinctive of the person. Ingrid loves information, and when she is driving it's all about the podcasts. She fills the car with historical and literary insights. Tom is a theologian at heart. He loves to discuss fine points of doctrine, how the whole Bible fits together, and how the church has understood these great theological truths. Taylor emphasizes transformation. She always directs the conversation back to real life, to the practical outworking of what all their discussion means.

Together these three friends create something that is stronger, richer, and more beautiful than what any one of them could accomplish individually. Together these three approaches to reading Scripture—informational, theological, and transformational—provide a robust and meaningful path for knowing God through the study of the Bible.

But no road trip would be complete without the delicious and spontaneous side trips. Throughout the three legs of our journey, led in turn by Ingrid, Tom, and Taylor, we are also going to pause at a few exits to eat and to ponder some beautiful things. These side trips aren't directly in the path of our destination, but they're not mere detours either. They are enriching moments that will provide a kind of experiential glue to the whole journey. And surprisingly, when we look back on the journey as a whole, we will see that these side trips were really connected all along. They all relate to the super-sized question of how we know anything (the fancy word for that is *epistemology*). Like any good side trip, therein lies the real adventure.

So let's begin. Come and see.

The First Stage of the Journey

Informational Reading with Ingrid

On this first leg of our journey, Ingrid is in charge. She's vivacious and vigorous and always fun to be around. When you're with Ingrid, you know it! She's passionate about knowledge, and she loves to share it with others. She's a great friend to have driving for the first stage: we know that we will be headed in the right direction, and the trip will be enriched by what she brings to our discussion.

For Ingrid, it's all about information. Her chosen podcasts and conversation fill the car with information of all sorts—historical, literary, and logical. As we learn from Ingrid how to read Scripture, we will grow in knowledge and skills that relate to gaining and integrating information. Ingrid will also lead us on two fascinating side trips about how maps enable us to see and how our imagination of the world shapes our interpretation of it.

 ORIENTATION

The informational aspect of reading the Bible refers to the fact that Scripture contains content that informs our minds and understanding. Scripture is *more* than informational content, certainly, but it is not less than this. God speaks to us in many ways, and we know things in many ways—experientially, emotionally, relationally. But one essential way that we know things is cognitively or through our minds. And our cognitive faculties work on content or information.

To read Scripture rightly, then, we must focus on the information it provides that is outside of us, not generated by us. This focus on Scripture's content entails a wide range of knowledge and the development of some important skills. Many tools can and should be in our informational interpretation tool box. These include understanding the historical and cultural background of Scripture, knowing something about language and how it works, developing literary interpretation skills, and recognizing different genres within Scripture.

Filling Up the Tank

Before we begin, let's first pause to get some gas (our friends can't yet afford a Tesla), and then we'll set off on our journey.

Ingrid gives the first words of her driving time to her beloved Eugene Peterson: "The more 'spiritual' we become, the more care we must give to exegesis. The more mature we become in the Christian faith, the more exegetically rigorous we must become. This is not a task from which we graduate."[1]

What does it mean to be more "exegetically rigorous"? *Exegesis* is the act of interpreting or drawing out the meaning of a Bible passage. Thus, to be exegetically rigorous means to engage in a detailed study of Scripture, its background, language, and history. This may sound like something a stodgy old professor might say, a sentiment that feels like a blaring loudspeaker from the ivory tower far removed from real life.

But the person who penned this quote, Eugene Peterson, was one of our generation's greatest pastors and leaders in spiritual formation.[2] Exegetical rigor and spirituality are not opposites, according to Peterson, but intimate friends. Peterson challenges us to make sure we are always doing *more* than rigorous exegesis—that we are also engaging in theological and transformational reading. But he understands that spiritual study of the Bible is never *less* than a detailed, careful reading. The more spiritual we are, the more we will give ourselves to watchful and meticulous study of the Bible. Even though spirituality and rigorous study of the Bible are often thought of as contrary to each other today, Peterson is saying what the great Christian tradition has always said.

Now for some people, the idea that rigorous study of the Bible (exegesis) is essential for *all* Christians might sound like an attempt at job security for people with PhDs in theology. Some might be concerned that this takes the Bible away from the average, church-going reader and requires that we all attend seminary and become learned experts on the nitty-gritty details of the Bible. For other readers, however, this idea is perfectly acceptable. Being academic and rigorous in our study of the Bible doesn't sound scary or bad, but exciting.

Whatever your perspective, I want to convince you that exegetical rigor is not something to shun, dismiss, or disdain. The reason is simple: if we are to grow in knowledge, wisdom, and love, we need to benefit from information that we don't currently have. The Bible records God's speech that doesn't originate from us. Therefore, to hear thoughts other than our own, we need to learn to listen attentively, to seek to gain information other than what we already possess.

But you might still wonder why learning God's thoughts takes exegetical rigor. Can't we just read the Bible and see what it says? Well, yes, we can and should read the Bible and see what it says. And at the end of our journey, we will see that this kind of simple and receptive reading is where we want to end up. But we also need to recognize that the Bible comes to us over a significant distance of time, culture, language, and worldview. We often need help to understand what the Bible is saying, and this is where a careful informational study of the Bible comes in.

We know that communication between spouses and friends often results in misunderstanding. Amplify this potential break-down of communication across languages, cultures, physical space, and thousands of years, and we can easily *mis*understand what the Bible is saying. Maybe even more disconcerting, it is shockingly easy to misunderstand the Bible *and not to even realize we are doing so*! Having lived in the United Kingdom for a few years, I can testify that unknown mistakes can happen when using American English in a British English context (and vice versa). One can blithely use words with very different meanings—such as *pants, sacked, boot, mad, jumper,* or *vest* to name just a few— and be completely unaware. (Even worse is misusing words that you don't realize have sexual meanings!) Exegetical rigor helps us avoid some of these missteps.

Hear me clearly: I'm not saying that we should think of the Bible as distant and incomprehensible. These are God's words, and God is always present and happy to speak to us. But wax tends to grow in our ears. Hear Peterson again:

> These words given to us in our Scriptures are constantly get-ting overlaid with personal preferences, cultural assumptions, sin distortions, and ignorant guesses that pollute the text. The pollutants are always in the air, gathering dust on our Bibles, corroding our use of the language, especially the language of faith. Exegesis is a dust cloth, a scrub brush, or even a Q-tip for keeping the words clean.[3]

So rigorous study of the Bible is wise and practical. We need a good informational reading strategy to clean off these pollutants and to clear out our ears.

We also need exegetical rigor for a more spiritual reason: it is a matter of *love.* As Peterson points out, the truly spiritual leaders of old were always master exegetes because they loved God and wanted to hear from him—not just have their own self-generated, self-centered "spirituality." "Exegesis is an act of love. It loves the one who speaks the words enough to want to get the words right. It respects the words enough to use every means we have to get the words right. Exegesis is loving God enough to stop and listen carefully to what he says."[4]

Thus, when we give ourselves to the intensive, rigorous study of Scripture (not always an easy task!), we are doing so out of respect and love for our Creator and Redeemer God. Thorough and even laborious study of Scripture is motivated by affection and the greatest human desire possible: to know and love God more. This is not the stuff of dry, arid "academics." Rather, learning to read in an informational way is like the kind of natural affectionate attention that avid sports fans give to learning their favorite players' names and stats. It's like the attention and energy that any lovers of horses or sports cars or fountain pens or mountain climbing give to their area of passionate interest.

But we have not yet really explained what this exegetical rigor is referring to. This is what Ingrid brings to our conversation. This love-based, willing-to-work-hard rigor in reading is what we are calling the *informational* type of reading. But what does this consist of, what does it require, and what does it look like? What exactly does Ingrid want us to embrace?

We will explore three aspects of a good informational reading of Scripture. These three aspects are (1) using a three-avenues approach to interpretation, (2) developing a sensitivity to different literary genres; and (3) recognizing (and avoiding) some common exegetical mistakes. As we travel on the path of developing these three skills, we'll also take a couple of fascinating side trips.

Reading through Three Avenues

A certified plumber or master electrician must learn a panoply of small skills to be able to function well: how to sweat copper pipe, how to set up a circuit box, how to fix the leak in a PVC sink trap, how to prevent aluminum wiring from causing a fire. So too, a good informational reader must learn reading skills in several areas to gain experience with different types of approaches to interpretation. I like to describe this as learning to read through *three avenues*.

We can describe these three avenues or routes as reading (1) behind the text, (2) in the text, and (3) in front of the text. Here's the basic idea for each of these reading habits:

- *Behind the text:* This kind of reading focuses on gaining information about the language, history, culture, geography, and worldview of the times and people of the Bible.
- *In the text:* This kind of reading pays attention to how the Bible functions as literature, learning skills that help us become better readers.

13

- *In front of the text:* This kind of reading listens to how those who have gone before us have read the same Bible, seeking to learn from the perspectives and insights of others.

Let's drill down a bit more and look at how each of these three avenues contributes to our understanding.

Behind the Text

The Bible was written over a span of more than a thousand years in two languages (plus a smattering of a third). It was written by a wide variety of people living in places and cultures very different than our own. These gaps in time and place matter. People can read the Bible and make it mean whatever they want, of course. But if we want to be good readers, we need at least *some* rudimentary knowledge of the background *behind the text*.

While the basic message of the Bible is accessible without extensive background knowledge, some parts of it are quite obscure without some help, and other parts are prone to great misunderstanding. For example, when God says in Psalm 60:8 (and Ps. 108:9), "Over Edom I shall throw My shoe" (NASB 1995), the meaning is not immediately apparent to us. When we look at different English translations, we find a variety of renderings because of the obscurity of this metaphor. Some translations speak instead of casting a shoe (or sandal) *on* Edom. Regardless, without some help we are at a loss. A literal reading would require that we find where ancient Edom was and assume that at one time God tossed his foot apparel there.

A far better solution is to understand what this saying meant in its own time and place—namely, taking possession of or even conquering the land. This is based, from what we can tell, on the ancient custom of throwing down a sandal as a sign of taking occupancy of a place. We could engage in further worthwhile exploration. It would be beneficial to think about the significance of Edom (which later is called Idumea) as part of the remaining unconquered territory of the original promised land. We might also ponder King David's role in completing this conquest where Israel earlier had failed.

Let's consider a slightly different kind of example, this time from the New Testament. We may ask what help background information can give us in interpreting a statement of Jesus in the book of Revelation. Jesus prophetically tells the Laodicean church that he would rather that they be hot or cold, but not lukewarm, lest he spit them out (Rev. 3:15–16). With nothing other than the text before them, many preachers have interpreted this to mean that God would rather we are either "on fire for Jesus" (hot) or distant and far away (cold), instead of being "lukewarm" church attendees who go through the motions with no heart for God. While this certainly will preach, we may rightly query whether this interpretation is true theologically. Would God *really* prefer that we avoid church and oppose him if we aren't completely devoted to him? It seems not. Being in church and hearing the word preached are the primary means by which lukewarm and cold people become "on fire" for God.

Knowing a bit of the cultural and historical background behind Revelation 3:15–16 helps us figure this out. Perhaps this hot-cold-lukewarm reference had a different meaning in the first-century Greco-Roman culture of Asia Minor than it has for us. Relevant background information could significantly affect our interpretation. As a good Bible dictionary or backgrounds commentary would explain, this phrase seems to refer to the Laodicean aqueduct system that delivered water at different temperatures. Hot water, delivered via one aqueduct system, was useful for cleaning and bathing. Cold water, delivered by another aqueduct, was for drinking. Laodicea's distance from the various hot and cold springs meant that its water was often neither hot nor cold but lukewarm, an undesirable state that meant it was useless for either of the purposes. Thus, Jesus's words reflect this cultural context. He is saying in effect, "Be useful!" This background material is not definitive; nevertheless, it's a good example of how behind-the-text information can be instructive and helpfully guide our interpretation.

TAKE A TURN AT THE WHEEL

Read Mark 6:6–12.s

The main point of this passage is clear enough—Jesus sent out his disciples to do the same kind of proclaiming and restoring work that he himself was engaged in. This is on-the-job training for the church's continuing work after Jesus returns to the Father.

But there's also a historical-cultural element in this story that may not be immediately clear. What did Jesus mean when he told his disciples to "shake off the dust" on their feet "as a testimony against" those who reject their message?

This is a cultural practice and expression that we need help understanding. You can certainly google this expression and find some helpful (and some unhelpful) explanations. But the best thing to do is to look at a reputable source like a Bible dictionary or a Bible backgrounds commentary. These can be found in print or in digital form. Here are a few good options:

- *The Dictionary of Biblical Imagery*, ed. Leland Ryken, James C. Wilhoit, and Tremper Longman III (Downers Grove, IL: InterVarsity Press, 1998).
- *Zondervan Illustrated Bible Backgrounds Commentary*, ed. Clint Arnold, 4 vols. (Grand Rapids, MI: Zondervan, 2002).
- *The Baker Illustrated Bible Background Commentary*, ed. J. Scott Duvall and J. Daniel Hays (Grand Rapids, MI: Baker, 2020).

You can look up the word "dust" or the phrase "shake off dust" and/or look for references to Mark 6:11.

In the Text

When we talk about the skill of learning to read *in the text*, we mean reading the Bible as literature. While Christians believe in the divine inspiration of the Bible, this does not mean that the Bible simultaneously ceases to be literature. The best understandings of the doctrine of inspiration speak of the Holy Spirit guiding humans—living in space and time—to use human words to communicate God's message. The Bible was not dictated to people who were in a trance. The Bible was not discovered as angelically inscribed tablets buried in the ground. God spoke to and through people who wrote Holy Scripture. Divine inspiration means the things written in Scripture are authoritative and trustworthy, *not* that they are magical or cease to be human writing.

This means that one helpful avenue for interpreting the Bible well is to learn how literature works. Thus, we should pay attention to how writers use literary techniques such as structured patterns, repetition, parallelism, and plot development to engage their readers and communicate their message.

EXAMPLE I

As an example, let's consider Psalm 1. Recognizing this as an intentionally structured poem (like all the psalms) helps us more accurately grasp its meaning and significance.

We can render Psalm 1 visually like this:

Blessed is the man
>   who walks not in the counsel of the wicked,
>   nor stands in the way of sinners,
>   nor sits in the seat of scoffers;

>   but his delight is in the law of the Lord,
>   and on his law he meditates day and night.

>   He is like a tree planted by streams of water
>   that yields its fruit in its season,
>   and its leaf does not wither.
>   In all that he does, he prospers.

The wicked are not so,

>   but are like chaff that the wind drives away.

Therefore the wicked will not stand in the judgment,
nor sinners in the congregation of the righteous;

for the LORD knows the way of the righteous,
but the way of the wicked will perish.

Let's make a few observations based on the literary structure of Psalm 1. Notice first that this psalm is built on a contrast of two different kinds of people—the blessed person (or better, "flourishing one") and the wicked. (I've highlighted this contrast by putting these two characters' lines on the far left.)

We are given a description of what the blessed or flourishing person's life looks like. We are told what he *doesn't* do and what he *does*. This flourishing person's life is not influenced or directed by an ungodly way of living. Notice that this is communicated through three parallel phrases. The bad guys are described with three different terms—*wicked, sinners, scoffers*; together they give us a composite picture that is the opposite of the flourishing person. And notice that these three lines also represent a downward progression—"walks" with the wicked becomes "stands" with sinners which becomes "sits" with scoffers. This is a subtle but powerful description of the way that negative influences increasingly lead someone astray.

By way of contrast, we are also told what the flourishing person *does*. He or she regularly meditates on God's word—that is, God's instructions and promises. God becomes this person's delight. Instead of basing his or her life on the ways of the world and its crooked wisdom, this person's heart, mind, and actions are guided by God's revelation.

Inhabiting the world this way (both what the person doesn't do and what he does) results in flourishing. Notice the beautiful metaphor used to describe the blessed person—a vibrant and verdant, fruit-laden tree whose roots are continually nourished by a refreshing stream.

All of this provides a stark contrast to the opposite kind of person, whom we meet two-thirds of the way through the poem. These people are described not as flourishing but as wicked. Note the singular versus plural contrast at play here: the flourishing person is described individually while the wicked are grouped together into a nameless mass.

Note also that we don't need a detailed description of what these wicked people are like. We can assume their actions are the opposite of the blessed one. But we are told in concrete terms the result of this way of life. In contrast to the rooted, flourishing tree, the wicked person's labor and life are merely windblown chaff. Rather than being part of the assembled community of the righteous ones (God's people), they will face judgment and loss.

Our psalm ends with a straightforward statement that once again clearly contrasts the two types of people: "The LORD knows the way of the righteous, but the way of the wicked will perish" (Ps. 1:6).

Now anyone reading this psalm could reach some of these same ideas. But paying attention to its composition as a piece of literature makes these insights pop off the page. This poem isn't a mere random series of statements; instead it communicates by juxtaposing two contrasting ways of life and their subsequent outcomes. When we carefully observe the literary structure, we are able to mentally organize what the psalm is saying and how its parts fit together. Most importantly, note that these observations aren't the result of some secret knowledge, nor do they require an elaborate theological education. These insights come from slowing down, paying attention, and asking questions about structure. This is a big part of what it means to read the Bible as real literature.

TAKE A TURN AT THE WHEEL

Read Psalm 8.

How is this psalm structured? Are there repeated phrases? Type or write out this short psalm and try indenting lines to indicate the structure. If 8:1 and 8:9 frame the whole psalm, how do these statements relate to the other verses?

EXAMPLE 2

Let's consider another example of paying attention to the Bible as literature, this time from the New Testament. We can gain a lot of in-the-text insight as we learn to pay attention to how the Gospel writers intentionally structure the order of the stories about Jesus. Here we are not talking about how a story itself is told (though that is important as well). Instead, we are pulling up a level and paying attention to how the Gospel writers have chosen to situate various stories next to one another. This is what I like to call the "divine crop circles"—the patterns in the field of the text that can only be seen when you get to a higher altitude and look at more than the individual stories.

We find unexpected meaning and significance when we look at the patterns of the stories—and not just at the stories themselves.

This is reading with an in-the-text literary sensitivity. As we read this way, we discover that the Gospel writers teach us about Jesus not only through specific narratives but also through the way multiple narratives are fitted together into a larger picture.

For example, the order of the assorted stories in Matthew 14–16 is no accident. The pattern, not just the individual accounts, proves to be theologically significant. First, we are told about the gruesome and cowardly murder of God's prophet, John the Baptist, at a drunken feast at Herod's palace (Matt. 14:1–12). After this, Jesus miraculously feeds thousands of needy people in the wilderness (14:13–21). Following this provision of bread, Jesus walks on water and reveals himself to his disciples as the Son of God (14:22–33). The religious leaders from Jerusalem then come and challenge Jesus because he doesn't follow their traditional rules about handwashing when eating (15:1–20). Then in sharp contrast to these faithless Jewish leaders, a Gentile woman is commended for her great faith in Jesus and granted the healing she desires (15:21–28). Jesus continues to teach and heal many people (15:29–31) and then performs another miraculous wilderness feeding in a Gentile area (15:32–38). He then crosses the sea once more (15:39), after which the religious leaders challenge him again (16:1–4). This leads to a discussion between Jesus and his disciples about the meaning of bread and his conflict with the religious leaders (16:5–12). Finally, we reach one of the most important texts in the Gospels, the Caesarea Philippi confession; the moment when the disciples clearly see and acknowledge that Jesus is the Messiah (16:13–20).

Is your head spinning yet? Did you get all that? I understand if you didn't. It would be tempting to merely read these stories one after another and never attempt to see any connection. After all, each story by itself offers rich ideas and teachings. But there's also something more going on. When we pull up to a higher altitude and observe these stories as a group, we begin to see movements and patterns that teach us something more.

Here's a table to help us look at the sequence of stories:

Stories in Matthew 14–16

Text	Story
Matthew 14:1–12	The death of John at Herod's feast
14:13–21	Jesus's miraculous feeding of the five thousand
14:22–33	Jesus's miraculous walking on water
15:1–20	The Jewish leaders challenge Jesus about their traditions regarding eating
15:21–28	A Canaanite woman shows great faith and is healed
15:29–31	Jesus heals many people in a Gentile area
15:32–38	Jesus's miraculous feeding of the four thousand
15:39	Jesus crosses the water
16:1–4	The Jewish leaders challenge Jesus about his authority
16:5–12	Jesus explains what the feeding and bread mean
16:13–20	The confession of Jesus as the Christ

Do you perceive any patterns? First look at the *repetitions*. Notice how many of these events and stories center on food. John's death happens at a feast. There are two wilderness feedings. The religious leaders challenge Jesus about their traditions concerning eating, and he responds in kind. Then Jesus explains himself to his disciples by referring to the feedings and the baskets of loaves collected. Not only are many of these stories about food but the two parallel accounts of miraculous feeding occur among two different people groups, Jews and Gentiles. And notice that both of the wilderness feedings are followed by Jesus's crossing over a body of water, one crossing being strikingly miraculous.

Now look at the *contrasts* built into the sequence of stories. There is a stark disparity between King Herod's opulent and decadent feast (resulting in the death of God's prophet) and King Jesus's humble and miraculous feeding in the wilderness (resulting in blessing for thousands of the poor and destitute). Notice that following this gracious wilderness provision for the people of the land, the Jerusalem-based leaders—instead of being happy that Jesus helped the poor—are unhappy that his disciples didn't wash their hands. The irony and pettiness is palpable. The sharp contrasts continue with a *Canaanite* woman juxtaposed with the Israelite leaders. There were no physical Canaanites left in Jesus's day; this is a throwback reference to the evil opponents of God's people when they entered the promised land. This perceptive foreign woman shows great faith in Jesus and is commended by God, but the Jewish religious leaders are shown to be opposed to God.

Finally, we note an *escalation* in these stories that culminates in the crystal clear revelation that Jesus is the Christ (the anointed King) and the Son of God. The miracles, teachings, and conflicts that precede this moment could be interpreted in a number of ways. Matthew makes clear that all of these events point to Jesus's royal power.

So what do we do with all of this? The ten-thousand-foot-divine-crop-circles perspective helps us see an ideogram we could not perceive at the ground level. The repetitions, contrasts, and sequence help us discern a deeper story being evoked and a bigger picture being painted. Specifically, we see Jesus the King of Israel as the one who brings a new and final exodus for both

Jewish and Gentile people, even amid the foolish opposition of the Jewish leadership. Bread in the wilderness, miraculous water crossings, reference to a Canaanite woman, welcoming of the poor and foreigners, humble faith in contrast to the Jewish leadership—all of this communicates that something bigger and deeper is happening. Jesus is the agent of a radically new era of God's redemptive work. He is, as the culminating story shows, the Christ, the Son of the living God!

Could you get this from simply reading the individual stories? No. Each story has its own meaning and application. But when they are taken together, a yet deeper meaning is communicated. This is the power of learning to pay attention to the Bible as theological literature.

TAKE A TURN AT THE WHEEL

Look over Matthew 21:23–22:46.

Let me jumpstart your thinking. Notice that this section is about Jesus's authority being questioned by the ones in authority, the religious leaders.

After the introduction in 21:23–27, count the stories between 21:28–22:46. How many are there? Is there a pattern to them? Are there repeated phrases or ideas? (Ignore the chapter break at 22:1.) How does this section escalate, and how does it conclude? What is the relationship between the introduction and the conclusion?

In Front of the Text

So far Ingrid has helped us see that good reading involves understanding issues *behind the text* of Scripture (acquiring historical, cultural, etc., background knowledge), as well as issues *in the text* (reading the Bible as literature). We can also read *in front of the text*. Such in-front-of-the-text reading focuses on how other people have read the Bible over time. In this avenue of reading, we consider how the text has been received by others and what effect it has had. This matters because we all read with our own blind spots, limitations, assumptions, and prejudices. Paying attention to what other readers have seen is a wise and fruitful approach to becoming better interpreters.

My beloved uncle used to quip that a day is never wasted if you can use a German word, so here is yours for today: *Wirkungsgeschichte* [vir-kung-ge-shick-te]. This awesome word refers to the history of the effects of a text. That is, we can ask, how has a text been utilized and applied by people in particular situations throughout history? This is helpful in enabling us to see aspects of a text that we may not have considered. For example, a *Wirkungeschichtliche* reading of Matthew 26–27 could examine how Johann Sebastian Bach used this story in his musical oratorio about Jesus's suffering and death. Bach's famous and powerful *Matthäus-Passion* (*St. Matthew Passion*) retells the last days of Jesus's earthly life in musical and vocal form. Bach faithfully and creatively presents Jesus in dialogue with his enemies and his disciples, weaving together insights from other portions of Scripture with vibrant and rich music. By paying attention to this interpretation of Matthew 26–27, our understanding and appreciation of Matthew's version of the story is enhanced.

Another example of music effectual history is George Frideric Handel's beautiful oratorio *Messiah*. Handel retells the birth of Jesus by skillfully interweaving it with many Old Testament prophecies, set to a potent musical score. *Messiah* is not only interpretively insightful but also aesthetically pleasing. It is delightful to observe how the solo tenor sings a series of oscillating notes on the word "crooked" in the citation from the KJV of Isaiah 40:4 and then a solid note for "plain" when describing the coming Messiah's work.[5] By slowing down and paying attention to these examples of *Wirkungsgeschichte*, our attentiveness to the text is deepened and expanded.

Another kind of in-front-of-the-text reading is called reception history, where we learn how different people have applied texts in their own cultural contexts. For example, one could examine how slave owners in the antebellum American South wrongly used biblical texts to support their practices, along with how other Christians used the same Bible to argue against slavery and the slave trade (such as William Wilberforce in England).

Reception history also helps us trace the origins/influences of certain assumptions that we have about biblical texts. For example, in both Jewish and Christian history, Genesis 3 was interpreted in a way that emphasized Eve's inferiority as a woman. Jewish authors like Philo and ben Sira suggest that Eve's sin was due to her gender, and Christian theologians often did the same. In medieval Europe, interpreters suggested that the devil appeared to Eve in the form of a woman. This idea began to appear in many works of art including Michelangelo's Sistine Chapel. Even today, advertisers often identify Eve with temptation by using images of snakes wrapped around nude women.[6] Reception history opens our eyes to see that the ways we read biblical texts are often assumptions influenced by traditional interpretations. This is not necessarily bad, but tracing these influences can make us more astute interpreters.

Broadly speaking, both *Wirkungsgeschichte* and reception history are part of the larger in-front-of-the-text category called the history of interpretation (a reading habit we'll return to when Tom is driving). Looking at how other people have interpreted and preached biblical texts over the course of history gives us insight into how we can better read these same texts. An important part of interpreting Jesus's Sermon on the Mount (Matt. 5–7), for example, is looking at its history of interpretation. There are significant differences between how Augustine, Thomas Aquinas, Martin Luther, John Calvin, and Charles Spurgeon read this passage. We experience great gain in our own interpretation when we wrestle with issues explored by earlier interpreters, such as how the Beatitudes relate to the gifts of the Spirit (see Matt. 5:2–12), what it means for Jesus to "fulfill" the law (see 5:17), or who the "pigs" are before whom we are not to cast our "pearls" (see 7:6).

The riches available to us in the history of interpretation are almost innumerable. This kind of in-front-of-the-text reading is one of the greatest resources we have before us as we embark on the journey of knowing God through Scripture.

TAKE A TURN AT THE WHEEL

How did ancient interpreters understand Jesus's command to "sell your possessions, and give to the needy" (Luke 12:33 // Matt 19:21)? They had a lot of interesting and challenging things to say. But how can we find this out?

Stepping into the broad and fast-moving river of the history of interpretation can be overwhelming. We often need help from knowledgeable experts in this area. A great book that introduces this topic and gives good examples of the history of interpretation is David Paul Parris's *Reading the Bible with Giants: How 2000 Years of Biblical Interpretation Can Shed New Light on Old Texts.*[7]

One of the best things we can do to read Scripture in this way is to consult older commentaries, especially from the first several centuries of the church. Thankfully, many of the commentaries by the church fathers have been translated into English. These are often also collected together and organized by biblical books, resulting in a commentary that records what many ancient interpreters said about a text. Many of these volumes can be found for the Old and New Testaments in the Ancient Christian Commentary on Scripture series by InterVarsity Press. More broadly, the Christian Classics Ethereal Library (ccel.org) is a free online resource that provides translated books of countless church fathers—commentaries as well as other works.

Spend a little time looking at what earlier interpreters said about Luke 12:33 (// Matt 19:21). After you've done so, you can also check out a little article I wrote on this issue.[8]

YOU ARE HERE

The First Stage: Informational Reading with Ingrid
- Reading through Three Avenues
- **Side Trip 1: Maps and Seeing**
- Understanding Different Literary Genres
- Side Trip 2: Reading in St. Petersburg (and Other Places)
- Avoiding Common Interpretive Mistakes

Side Trip 1: Maps and Seeing

I have been a licensed operator of cars for more than thirty-five years now and have driven untold miles. I have also (mostly) successfully taught my six children to drive. That part was a little stressful but easy enough. What has been more difficult is teaching them where places in Louisville, Kentucky, are in relation to one another. My otherwise intelligent children simply don't think in terms of the compass points and the spatial relations of Shelbyville Road to Fourth Street like I do. When I've tried to explain where things are geographically, they are blank eyed and impatient. "I'll just put it in my phone" is the exasperated answer I get. When my kids plan to go to a friend's house, they think of the destination in terms of minutes away, and they think of the drive in terms of the turns dictated by their phones. That is how many people think now.

I finally realized that most people under thirty don't care about spatial relations because they don't see the world the same way I do. When I think of Chicago or Louisville or Orlando, I see them in my mind's eye on a two-dimensional, color map with roads and points of interests with me looking down from above. This is because when

I learned to drive we had no digital GPS tools but only a Rand McNally Road Atlas. This 18x24-inch book of color maps had to be consulted to figure out which roads and interstates—combined with a diligent watching of road signs—would enable you to get someplace new and unfamiliar. Without an atlas you were lost and dependent on potentially inaccurate oral directions at a gas station.

It is not an overstatement to say that we each *think about* the space we live in differently because we *see* it differently. The type of maps we use enable us to see the world in a certain way.

The making of a map of any sort—whether AT&T's fiber coverage in Cincinnati, migratory flight paths that cross oceans, favorite movies per US state, or the twenty-two countries that Great Britain has not invaded—enables us to see our indescribably rich and complex world in certain ways.

No map can be comprehensive or even come close. Even a perfectly scaled map of a tiny area must make a myriad of choices about what to include and not include: bird song, utility lines, dog markings, number of acorns. Most information must be left out. An entirely comprehensive map of an area would be the world itself, which is what we already have. Maps exist to enable us to see something about our world, to see it in a particular way, to see connections and relations between mere data points within the story and song of the world.

In 1933 Harry Beck changed the world of urban mapping with his unique new graphic representation of the London subway system. Before Beck, the maps of the London Underground were accurate in giving the distance and direction of train lines but, it turned out, actually too accurate. There was simply too much information for people to interpret and use these subway maps. Beck's revolutionary mapmaking involved a simplified and attractive representation (the characteristics of a good map) of the different train lines—color coded and with neat angles. The distances and length of stops are not represented in his maps, nor is information about neighborhoods. But riders are given what they need to successfully navigate the Underground: which train lines stopped where and in what order. This approach to urban transportation maps has now been adopted around the world. According to Peter Turchi, what Beck's cartography shows is that "the most accurate map, and the most detailed map, is not necessarily the best map."[9]

The most important thing to learn from Beck is that maps enable us to see things in a certain way, often by blank space and deselection as well as by curated selection of information. Mapmaking enables a perspective that is never coextensive with reality (only reality itself is that), but its selectivity empowers us to understand in a certain way.

What does this have to do with being a good Bible reader? Understanding our creaturely limited perspectives on the world invites us to humility. Our inevitably limited understanding reminds us of what is most true about us: we are not God. Our perspective, insights, and perceptions are imperfect and incomplete, even at our best moments.

For example, when we determine what we think is a good interpretation of a text, we should not assume that these verses are now locked up and solved. If later we see something we did not see before or hear someone teach or preach something about the text that is different than what we thought, a posture of humility is open to consider an adjustment in our thinking. We are not to be "tossed to and fro by the waves and carried about by every wind of doctrine" (Eph 4:14), but neither are we to hold on to a sacred cow of interpretation, even if it was personally meaningful to us before. Recognizing our limits as knowers and readers invites us

to a continual posture of humility and teachability as we continue
our lifelong journey of knowing God through Scripture.

> **YOU ARE HERE**
>
> The First Stage: Informational Reading with Ingrid
> - Reading through Three Avenues
> - Side Trip 1: Maps and Seeing
> - **Understanding Different Literary Genres**
> - Side Trip 2: Reading in St. Petersburg (and Other Places)
> - Avoiding Common Interpretive Mistakes

Understanding Different Literary Genres

While Ingrid is driving, information is the primary tone and focus
of our discussion. As we continue our journey toward understanding God, Ingrid offers us three information-focused skills. The first
skill we considered was the three avenues of reading (behind the
text, in the text, and in front of the text). The second skill involves
learning to interpret the Bible according to the different literary
genres that it contains.

The word *genre* refers to a type and style of writing that can be
distinguished from other types. As soon as we browse a *Calvin and
Hobbes* comic, the *Wall Street Journal*, a biblical commentary, a
teen vampire novel, and a college biology textbook, we know that
these are examples of different literary *genres*, even if we're unfamiliar
with that word. These diverse types of writing use various modes of
communicating for different purposes. Each genre creates an expectation in readers and requires a unique set of skills to understand.

The Bible is God's revelation of himself, thus making it *more* than a mere human book. But it is not *less* than a human book. The books of the Bible were written by a wide range of people over a large span of time in many cultures and in three different languages (Hebrew, Aramaic, and Greek). Moreover, since the Bible was written by real humans living in real human cultures, it contains a variety of literary genres. As one scholar says, "God does not speak his word through Scripture in a way that bypasses human creatures, but in a way that works through them."[10]

As a result, we must recognize that to read the Bible well entails paying attention to many human elements that will enable us to interpret in the best way. This involves historical and cultural information as well as literary analysis as discussed above. This also means learning the ways that people develop genres as culturally embedded modes of writing.

Rather than thinking about the Bible as a *book*, we can more helpfully view it as a *library*. The Bible-library has walls, its contents are curated, and it has a unified message—this is where the idea of *canon* comes in (more on this below). But imagine if you went to a library that had books only on one topic, only for a certain age level, and only written in one particular style. Although that might be helpful in a narrow way, such a library could never serve you for the complexity and the span of your life.

Thankfully, the Bible is rich, varied, and more expansive than that. The biblical library contains many genres: legal instruction, poetry, apocalyptic (a kind of fantasy literature), wisdom sayings, instructional letters, strongly worded sermons, songs, and *lots* of stories. Together these beautifully and richly testify to God's nature, heart, and mission in the world.

In recent decades a lot of books on biblical interpretation have focused on the skill of understanding genre interpretation, so we need not reinvent the wheel. If you desire, you can find more details in other places.[11] Here we will briefly explore seven different genres found in Scripture and how best to interpret them.

Narratives or Stories

People who are unfamiliar with the Bible often assume that it primarily contains lists of things to do and not do. This is understandable as indeed the sacred books of many other religions do focus on instruction and morality. But one of the most striking and important things about the Bible from a genre perspective is recognizing that the vast majority of its pages tell *stories*. Or, to use the more technical genre term, most of the Bible consists of *narratives*. Depending on how one calculates it, the Bible is about 70–80 percent narrative.

The narrative portions of Scripture span the whole of the Bible, both the Old and New Testaments. Not all narratives function in exactly the same way, and we can distinguish, for example, some differences between Old Testament histories and New Testament biographies (the Gospels). But for our purposes we will concentrate on the basic way in which all stories function.

In short, narratives are best interpreted by recognizing that, unlike legal documents or teaching instructions, stories communicate through means of plot, characters, and dialogue. The *plot* of a story is the path or journey that the story takes as it unfolds. Key to a plot is some kind of tension or conflict. Without tension a plot cannot exist, and without a plot a story cannot exist. When we say colloquially, "The plot thickens," we are unconsciously acknowledging the reality that some conflict, tension, or problem makes a story meaningful. And the deeper the tension, the greater the possible resolution—thereby resulting in greater meaningfulness and beauty. The plot of a picture book about a kid losing a plastic trinket is inherently thinner than the complex characters and plot of the seven-volume Harry Potter series.

Stories also need *characters*. Characters in the Bible are usually humans, although Balaam's donkey, angels, snakes and dragons, and of course God himself also make appearances. Characters interact with one another, causing and/or experiencing the tension that makes a story. The characters carry the story along and serve as types or exemplars of different ways of being in the world, for good or for bad. Often human characters are presented in contrasting pairs for our instruction. We see good choices and bad choices and their consequences, inviting us to think about our own lives. The most important character in the Bible is God himself. He is the beginning and end of the grand story of the Bible, and he is present in every story, with varying degrees of explicitness. Remembering that the Bible is primarily about God's activity helps us guard against reading the biblical stories as *only* about humans and our individual choices of morality. The biblical stories do relate to us in this human and practical way, but God's role is always central.

In the midst of a plot, characters speak to each other, to themselves, and to God. We call this *dialogue*. When a story breaks from action to talking, we should pay close attention. Dialogue in biblical narratives is typically where the gold of the story is found.

Recognizing that narratives communicate through the means of plot, characters, and dialogue helps us to be better readers of Scripture. The benefit of genre analysis is that we learn to interpret a type of literature in accord with how it works. Practically, this means that when we read narratives in the Bible, we should not isolate verses or portions of a story from the unfolding plot, nor should we interpret characters' words or actions apart from the story. Stories are a complete package and must be taken as a whole. You wouldn't pick up a novel and read just a line from somewhere in the middle. You may be able to comprehend the English sentence, but it won't really make sense unless you understand how this sentence is part of the plot and character development. So too with biblical stories. Good genre analysis teaches us to pay attention to how the story works.

TAKE A TURN AT THE WHEEL

Read 1 Samuel 17:1–58.

This famous story of David and Goliath is not just for children. The more we read it the better it gets. The books of 1–2 Samuel are some of the most enjoyable and insightful of the biblical narratives. To interpret 1 Samuel 17 well it is, of course, best to start at chapter 1 and read through. But even if you don't do that just now, you can read the narrative of David and Goliath well by paying attention to plot, characters, and dialogue.

What is the plot of the story? What is the most tense point in the narrative?

Who are the characters? List them. What role does each play in the plot?

Reread the dialogue. What does the discourse of the characters tell us about what the author is trying to communicate to us?

The Law

The first five books of the Old Testament are often called the Pentateuch or simply "the Law." The "law" can also be a shorthand reference for the old covenant—that is, God's special relationship with Israel. In addition we find in the Bible many commands that we call "laws." The multiple uses of the word *law* can be very confusing when we read the Bible and think about its contents. Even more problematic, it turns out that "law" is not really the best translation for the Hebrew word, *torah*, at play here. Rather, *torah* means "instructions." And in the Bible, specifically, it means *covenantal* instructions, that is, instructions for how we are to live in light of the loving and gracious relationship (covenant) God is making with humanity.

Thus, the first thing to observe about interpreting the law portions of the Bible is that we are not dealing with God as a stuffy, disengaged, nonrelational courtroom judge. Rather, the law is the set of instructions for how to live rightly and well in personal relationship with God. The law or torah is God's gracious gift to his people *as part of a covenant relationship*. When the instructions for the covenant relationship are followed, life is full of shalom (Hebrew for *peace*) and flourishing.

Think of it like marriage, which is also a covenant. Marriage includes certain stipulations, sometimes stated explicitly, sometimes not. These are often expressed in vows made on the wedding day and hopefully remembered throughout the marriage. These stipulations include things like faithfulness and affection. The man and woman vow "to have and to hold from this day forward, forsaking all others, 'til death do us part." This is torah. A husband or wife could treat these instructions in a sterile, obligatory, even resentful way, but this would deny the fundamentally relational and loving context of the stipulations. So too in our relationship with God.

The laws of the Old Testament address the two aspects of our human existence: relationship with our Creator God and relationship with other created beings. All of God's instructions concern one or the other of these relationships. This can be seen in the most succinct summary of the Old Testament law of God, the Ten Commandments (Exod. 20:1–17). The Lord gave them to Moses on two stone tablets, which can be divided into relating properly to God (commandments 1–4) and relating properly to humanity (commandments 5–10). Jesus himself summed up the heart of God's instructions the same way, saying that the first and second greatest commandments are to love God and love others (Matt. 22:36–40).

So we must begin thinking about the law or torah as a genre that comes to us not negatively from the hand of an angry, distant God but as an invitation to full human flourishing through a relationship with him.

While this is an important starting point, it does not completely solve the biggest genre question regarding the law—that is, what role does the law continue to play in the Christian's life? Are the many instructions and commands we find in the Old Testament still binding on Christians who are part of a new covenant in Jesus Christ? This difficult issue has been debated since the earliest days of Christianity itself. Jesus addressed the question head-on in his famous Sermon on the Mount (Matt. 5–7). He said that he had not come to abolish the law, but neither were things remaining unchanged. He referred to this affirmation and transformation of the law as "fulfillment" (Matt. 5:17–19).

It is not possible here to fully explore what this Christian fulfillment of torah means. However, we can note one crucial observation that affects our genre interpretation: torah instructions are tied to a particular covenant between God and Old Testament Israel. According to both the Old and New Testaments, however, Christians are not members of the same covenant that God made with Moses and the Israelites (see especially Gal. 3). The Old Testament looked forward to a time when God would make a new and deeper covenant with humanity (Jer. 31:31–34). On the night before his death, Jesus told his disciples that he was making this new covenant through himself (Luke 22:20).

This means that while the law/torah is still the inspired word of God—valuable as a witness to who he is and how he relates to his creation—Christians are not part of this particular covenant given through Moses (see the contrast in John 1:17–18). Therefore, Christians are not bound by the minutiae of the law, whether instructions for animal sacrifice, guidance for addressing mold in your house, or dietary regulations. Instead, according to the fundamental Christian understanding, Jesus has inaugurated a new covenant that includes his followers by means of their spiritual union with him. Through Jesus's life, death, resurrection, and ascension, he has accomplished all that God requires of humans. Our covenant with God is now through Jesus Christ, and we follow "the law of Christ" (Gal. 6:2). Through the power of the Holy Spirit, Christians obey the stipulations of this new covenant.

This adherence to the new covenant includes a backwards rereading of the entirety of God's instructions through the lens of who Jesus is and what he taught. In short, our reading of the Old Testament law must be attentive both to how God revealed himself originally and how the new covenant teachings enable us to reread this revelation through Christ. We do not neglect or abolish the teachings of the law, nor do we read them apart from their covenantal context.

The law must be re-understood through the Son Jesus (see 1 Cor. 10:1–13; 2 Cor. 1:20; Heb. 1:1–3). For an introduction to what can be a complicated topic, see Thomas R. Schreiner's helpful book *40 Questions about Christians and Biblical Law*.[12]

Poetry and Proverbs

Humans create not only stories and rules but also poetry and proverbs. Poetic writing uses words in concentrated and imaginative ways to express experiences and emotions. Proverbs likewise use creative imagery and pithy insights to communicate wisdom, guiding people to a flourishing life.

The Bible contains lots of poetry throughout, but the most condensed portion is found in the Psalter, the book of one hundred fifty Hebrew psalms or songs. Similarly, proverbial sayings are located in much of the Bible, but the book called Proverbs is the most compressed form of these sayings. Even though poetry and proverbs are different literary genres, we can treat them together because they share this distinctive: they communicate through images and wordplay not through direct propositional instruction. Psalms and proverbs are *indirect* theological communication.

Psalm writers explore and express their experiences and emotions. Thus, God's inspired word contains not only from-the-mountain instructions but also from-the-earth expressions. The psalms convey the records of people who are grieving, rejoicing, questioning, and wondering—full of fear and full of faith. Poetry is the highest form of human language, trafficking in concentrated and creative images, which is precisely what is needed to communicate the whole gamut of human experiences. But poetry is always indirect. Psalms are not heavy-handed instruction but inspired human expression that we get to overhear from the next room. Therefore, we must be careful not to treat psalms as if they were primarily providing doctrinal teaching. This may happen in a secondary or inferred way. But if we treat poetry non-poetically we will miss its point and possibly over-interpret it. Psalms are meant to be vehicles for us to learn to express our own experiences of grief and praise. Our articulation is helped by other people of faith who have gone before us. Psalms are training wheels that teach us to ride the road of life, not instruction manuals on how to fix sprockets.

Similarly, we must recognize proverbial literature for what it is: generalized statements that communicate principles of wisdom. Wise principles are beneficial for guiding us in how to live *generally*. But life is messy and complex; thus no principle will apply in all situations. As it turns out, this is the essence of wise living—learning principles that provide guard rails for life but realizing that we must make wise decisions as unique situations arrive. Proverbs provide such general principles. They offer *neither* specific instructions that always apply *nor* covenantal promises from God. For example, in two verses right next to each other, Proverbs gives opposite instructions to be applied in different situations: "Answer not a fool according to his folly" (Prov. 26:4) and "Answer a fool according to his folly" (Prov. 26:5). Similarly, we must understand that a statement such as "Train up a child in the way he should go; even when he is old he will not depart from it" (Prov 22:6) is a generalized principle but not a specific covenantal promise. Such is the wisdom of proverbial literature—it guides us without robotically specifying what we should do in every situation. This is in fact what the life of wisdom looks like.

Prophetic Writing

God is gracious and loving. Because of this, he wants to reveal himself to his creatures. He has done this through raising up spokespersons who have declared his words. The Bible is simply the inscripturation, or writing down, of these revelations. Some of these speakers whom God has called are given the title "prophets." To modern ears, "prophecy" often connotes a message about the future. Indeed, the biblical prophets do sometimes predict and describe future events. But fundamentally, prophetic words are sermonic revelation more than prediction. They are calls from God to humanity about how to live now, not mere forecasts regarding the future. Scripture includes many prophetic messages, but they are most concentrated in what we call the Major and Minor Prophets in the Old Testament.[13]

Two key ideas help us interpret the genre of prophetic literature. The first idea overlaps with our discussion of poetry above. We may be surprised to learn that much of the prophetic writing is poetic in form—both in its structure and in its strong use of imagery. This does not mean that prophetic literature is indirect. It's often not, especially when God is rebuking injustice and corruption. But it does mean that, as with all poetry, an overly literal reading will often miss the point. The power of imaginative language is its aesthetic punch not its referentiality. That is, poetic prophecy makes a clear point by the use of a poignant image. We must concentrate on the intended message not the particular image. This is especially true when the prophets are envisioning the promised future. Descriptions of the future are often highly imaginative (though not imaginary)[14] and must be read as such.

The second key idea for interpreting the prophetic literature is the same matter we raised above regarding a Christian appropriation of the law. God's prophets were called to be covenant enforcement mediators. If they were true prophets, they were not speaking of their own accord, nor were they typically calling God's people to something new. Rather, they were rebuking their hearers for not obeying their covenant relationship with God. Therefore, prophetic messages must be interpreted within the covenant in which they are delivered. Such messages will always reveal the heart of God, but the specifics of their instruction are contained within a covenant. Thus, from the perspective of the new covenant, when reading the Old Testament prophets we must take the same nuanced and two-sided approach that we do toward the law. The writings of the prophets are still abidingly meaningful and instructive as part of God's revelation, yet their specific instructions do not *necessarily* apply directly to us because of our different covenantal relationship with God.

TAKE A TURN AT THE WHEEL

Read Hosea 6.

Hosea is one of the twelve Minor Prophets whose words are gathered into the section of the Old Testament we call the Twelve (Hosea–Malachi). The best approach is to read Hosea in its entirety, but if you want to just dip in, you can read chapter 6.

What do these prophetic words reveal about who God is and what he cares about? What do these words tell us about ourselves—our tendencies of heart, our limits, our sinfulness?

Concentrate on Hosea 6:6. How does this verse get picked up and used in Jesus's ministry? Look at Matthew 9:1–13 and then Matthew 12:1–8. How does reading Hosea inform what is happening in Matthew 9 and 12? How do Matthew 9 and 12, in turn, help us understand Hosea?

Epistles (Letters)

As we noted above, the bulk of the Old Testament consists of narrative or stories explaining God's activity in the world. The remainder of the Old Testament writings apply, explore, and reinforce that story. So too with the New Testament. The four Gospels and Acts make up the vast majority of the New Testament, and they are primary in terms of explaining God's revelation in Jesus Christ. But the remainder of the New Testament is also important in extending our understanding and application of these truths. The interplay of the Old Testament prophets to the Old Testament narratives is analogous to the relationship of the New Testament Epistles (or Letters) to the Gospels and Acts. Both groups are important, but they approach the task from different starting points.[15]

To interpret the epistle genre well, we can note a few important practices. First, it is best to read an epistle as a whole whenever possible. Reading larger chunks of Scripture in any genre is always a good idea, but for epistles this is especially important. A letter is sent as a direct communication with a particular purpose in mind. One can easily take lines of epistolary instruction out of context. In the same way that a sentence in an email or text could be greatly misconstrued without reading the whole message, so too many times epistles are treated as a grab bag or celestial claw-machine game where the Christian snatches a verse that looks shiny and attractive and takes it home without considering the literary context. When reading epistles we should think in terms of paragraphs not verses or sentences. Epistles communicate their messages through sustained discourse, not in proverb-sized, disconnected nuggets. So read each epistle as a whole.

Second, we should remember that reading a New Testament letter is like listening to one side of a phone conversation. If we know the person whose phone conversation we're hearing, we can probably make (mostly) good sense of what is being said. Nevertheless, there is always great potential to misunderstand. We might misconstrue the topic of the conversation, or we might not realize that there is unseen background to why the conversation is going the way it is. This means that we should always read epistles with humility, recognizing that we probably do not fully understand what is going on in the conversation. Even so, God is still gladly revealing himself to us through these historically situated letters (always remember 2 Tim. 3:16-17).

This latter observation relates to the third and most important insight. Epistles, much more than narratives, poetry, proverbs, or even the law, are *occasional* documents. This means that they are a type of literature written almost entirely in response to some specific occasion or situation the author needs to address. In this sense they are most like the Old Testament prophets. Of course, all literature is written from within and speaking to a particular culture because its human authors are situated in a particular time and place. But some writings are much more narrowly occasional than others. My list of errands to do today is more occasional than the book of classic poems sitting on my dining room table.

It is important to understand that this *occasional* nature of epistles does not in any way diminish their inspiration or authority; however, as a genre they need to be handled slightly differently. Specifically, when we interpret epistles, historical and cultural information will prove to be more significant to help us understand what is being said and how it applies to us. Because of their occasional nature, we need to understand more of the occasion at hand. Thankfully, we have at our disposal massive amounts of historical and cultural information in commentaries and reference works that can enable us to discern what the authors of the New Testament letters are communicating.

This last point raises the biggest dilemma for good epistle interpretation: how much of their message is culturally defined and constrained? The particular context of the New Testament Epistles is first-century, Mediterranean Greco-Roman and Jewish culture. Inevitably, then, there are aspects that don't necessarily transfer and apply directly to modern Christian readers in different cultures. Most Christians today (at least in Western culture) do not "greet one another with a holy kiss" despite it being apparently commanded twice in the New Testament (Rom. 16:16; 2 Cor. 13:12). Nor do most contemporary female believers wear head coverings during church, despite a lengthy exposition regarding this in 1 Corinthians 11:2–16. Certainly some Christians do follow those commands while other faithful, Bible-believing Christians don't. The reason some Christians don't wear head coverings is that while they still recognize there is some principle to learn from the instruction, the specific form of application is culturally conditioned. God's word is to be obeyed, but it will not always look identical when the instructions are tied to particular, cultural habits. This doesn't make this literature less inspired or authoritative, but to read it well requires this cultural sensitivity.

The real difficulty becomes discerning which aspects of the instructions should be interpreted as culturally bound and which should not. For example, there is no small debate among evangelicals about whether Paul's instructions on the role of women in church (1 Tim. 2:11–12) fall into the same category as head coverings and holy kisses. These difficult interpretive decisions need to be handled and argued on a case-by-case basis; there is no one-size-fits-all solution. The key is a wise and humble wrestling that recognizes our need to be culturally sensitive interpreters while also acknowledging that we can be easily tempted to write off some teachings in Scripture because they do not fit with our desires or habits.

Parables

One of the most well-known things about Jesus's ministry is that he loved to teach in parables. Depending on how exactly we define a parable, approximately 35 percent of his teaching comes to us in this form. Biblical parables include allegorical stories, poetic images, similes, and metaphors. Jesus's teachings were memorable not only because they were often shocking and unexpected, but also because they used accessible analogies from agriculture, the marketplace, and real-life relationships.

Jesus wasn't the first person to teach with parables. There are parables scattered throughout the Old Testament, such as when the prophet Ezekiel described the Babylonian exile as a full-plumage eagle that snapped off the top of a cedar tree and planted it in a different city (Ezek. 17:2–10). Nathan the prophet used a parable to indict King David for his sins of seducing Bathsheba and killing her husband (2 Sam. 12:1–13). Teaching in parables is the purview of prophets and sages, two key roles that Jesus also played.

There is no "Book of Parables" in the Old Testament or New Testament. Most of the parables occur in collections peppered throughout the Gospels. Because they function in a special way, it is worth making a few comments about interpreting the genre of parables.

Our term *parable* refers to a wide range of forms of speech in Hebrew and Greek cultures including riddles, stories, pithy sayings, and allegories. Parables come in many shapes and sizes, and at times they function like narratives, like poems, like proverbs, and like apocalyptic literature. *Parable* is really a general term we use to describe a range of ways of speaking that all use analogy. Parables can be lengthy allegorical stories such as the parable of the sower, or they can be simple, pithy aphorisms such as "The kingdom of heaven is like treasure hidden in a field" (Matt. 13:44). The consistent element is that they all use some comparison or analogy.

As a result, the best practice for interpreting parables well is to pay attention to how the analogy is working. *What is the point of comparison and what seems to be the point being made by the comparison?* Sometimes there will be a summary statement such as "So the last will be first, and the first last" (Matt. 20:16) or "Thus he declared all foods clean" (Mark 7:19), making our job a bit easier. But whether or not such a statement is present, we should think in terms of how the comparison is working and not focus on minor details that are unrelated to the comparison.

For example, in Jesus's parable about the pearl of great price, a man sells everything he has to buy one great pearl (Matt. 13:45–46). Speculation about the price fluctuation of pearl prices in first-century Judaism is not going to serve the interpreter well. Nor will it be helpful to ponder what the man plans to do with this big pearl once he gets it. The point of the parable hinges on the analogy that it is worth selling lesser things to gain something of greater value. Jesus is clearly teaching that the kingdom of God is of greater value than anything else to us and that we should be willing to give up all else to obtain it.

Another important interpretive principle is paying attention to the literary context in which the parables are set. Parables by their nature are somewhat flexible in their meaning; they are "open" poetic texts that can communicate more than one idea, even as stories regularly do. As a result, we often discern a parable's specific application by paying attention to how the writer has set the parable in the flow of other teachings and sayings.

For example, the notoriously difficult parable of the laborers in the vineyard (Matt. 20:1–16) makes best sense when we look at the surrounding stories. This parable is a response to the disciples' question about their own future rewards from God relative to the future state of the rich young ruler (Matt. 19:16–30). The literary context around this parable shows us that the disciples, just like us, tended to compare themselves to one another (see also their spat about who will be greatest in the kingdom in 20:20–28). The parable challenges the disciples to see that God is free to do what he wants and to bless as he sees fit. The call to the disciples from the parable is that they must cease the comparison game with one another and recognize God for his great generosity.

TAKE A TURN AT THE WHEEL

Read Luke 15:1–32.

You're probably familiar with the third story in this series of parables, what we typically call the parable of the prodigal son. But notice that in Luke 15 Jesus gives us three related parables that build on one another.

What repeated patterns are there in these parables? What differences are there? What analogies are being made? Who do the different characters represent in the real world? Did you notice the addition in the third parable? We not only have a son who was lost and then found but also another son who never left and is now mad. What is the significance of this?

Apocalyptic Visions

The final genre to discuss is apocalyptic literature. The book of Revelation is the most famous example of apocalyptic in Scripture, but this genre also makes an appearance in significant portions of the Old Testament prophetic literature (e.g., Ezek. 38–39; Dan. 7–12) as well as in the Olivet Discourse in the Gospels (Mark 13 and parallels).

As with some of the other examples, apocalyptic actually contains a mixture of other genres. Apocalyptic literature typically employs poetic imagery and phrasing, may have narrative and epistolary portions, and regularly functions like a prophetic word of both warning and future hope. As a result, we must be sensitive and deft when reading apocalyptic literature, employing the skills and insights that apply to several other genres discussed above.

Answering two important questions is essential to interpreting apocalyptic well: Why is it written? How does it work? First, apocalyptic literature is typically written by a persecuted group in society that is seeking to encourage one another with the hope of a different future. This is true for everything from religious cults to nineteenth-century African slaves whose songs reflect an apocalyptic way of using language to conceal and to give hope. Jewish and Christian people in the Bible who experienced isolation and persecution used this genre as an important way to express their hope in God's coming kingdom. The persecution context and the future-hope focus explain why the style is typically image-heavy and poetic. Apocalyptic images function as indirect communication that speaks powerfully to insiders while concealing the content of the hope to the outsiders—the persecutors. Identity among a group of people is powerfully cultivated through a shared, image-laden language.

This understanding of the *why* leads us to understand the *how* of apocalyptic. This literature is written not so that the reader can decipher precisely what every poetic image means but rather so that we might be challenged and encouraged to diligence and persever- ance as we await God's full redemption. Apocalyptic literature is not to be read with a newspaper in hand so that we can figure out exactly whom Daniel or John identifies as the antichrist. Instead, the images are meant to inspire and affirm our longing for the time when God will set the world to right. Apocalyptic literature is not a secret code to be cracked but a memorable vision meant to build up hope by reminding us that God is in control of history and is actively at work bringing about his beautiful redemption.

Leg Stretch

This has been a long stretch of road, and we've covered a lot of miles. Ingrid has given us much help on the second skill needed to become good informational readers: understanding different literary genres. Let's pause for a moment, stretch our mental legs, and look back over the road we've just traversed. This discussion is important because when we read the Bible without sensitivity to the ways in which different genres communicate, there is the potential for misunderstanding what God is saying to us. Being aware of this hazard should not drive us to anxiety or paralysis in reading the Bible. God is happy to speak to us, and he *does* speak to us in and through our very imperfect understanding and inter- pretation. Nevertheless, our goal should always be to grow toward reaching the deepest, wisest, and most beneficial reading. And being sensitive to literary genres is one help along this journey. We can flip this around and say it more positively: when we can identify genre in our reading, we know what part of the Bible's library we're standing in, and we can more fully enjoy what each part of the Bible intends to communicate.

📍 **YOU ARE HERE**

The First Stage: Informational Reading with Ingrid
- Reading through Three Avenues
- Side Trip 1: Maps and Seeing
- Understanding Different Literary Genres
- **Side Trip 2: Reading in St. Petersburg (and Other Places)**
- Avoiding Common Interpretive Mistakes

Side Trip 2: Reading in St. Petersburg (and Other Places)

New Testament scholar Mark Allan Powell tells the story of a fascinating experiment he did in St. Petersburg, Russia.[16] The story actually begins in the United States when he was teaching the parable of the prodigal son (Luke 15:11–32). Powell did an exercise with his students that I do with mine now as well (and I recommend you try for yourself). He had them read this parable, recount it from memory, and then check to see what they missed. When he did this with his US students, only a very small percentage (about six percent) recalled Luke 15:14 with its reference to "a severe famine" afflicting the land where the wayward son was living. When he did the same exercise in St. Petersburg, however, he found that nearly all of the Russian students (eighty-four percent) included this detail in their recounting of the story.

Yet this was only part of what Powell found. He also discovered that the American and Russian students had rather different interpretations of what was going on in the story overall. The American students tended to see the prodigal son's problem as his foolish squandering of his wealth. The Russians, by contrast, interpreted the problem as the son's foolish desire to be independent of his family, to be self-sufficient, which became acutely problematic through the famine.

Powell insightfully notes that these different tendencies of interpretation are based on the distinct cultural and historical situations of the two groups of students. The Americans' interpretation reflects values common in a capitalistic society where individuals are seen as reaping what they sow with their lives for good or for bad. The Russians' interpretation likewise reflects their own more socialist and communal sensibilities, seeing the son break those conventions to his harm. Additionally, Powell surmises that the devastating siege of Leningrad (the name of St. Petersburg from 1924–91) during WWII was still remembered by the grandparents and great-grandparents of these students. Starvation and famine were a real part of the cultural memory of the Russians in a way not conceivable by the Americans.

So how does this help us become better readers of Scripture? These different interpretations of the parable are not completely contradictory and are not in competition with each other. The main ideas of the parable—that the father welcomes the wayward son and that the older brother is angry—are grasped by both groups of students. At the same time, both groups, situated in their own cultural contexts, provide certain insights into how best to read the story and feel its nuances.

Ingrid rightly emphasizes understanding the historical culture of the Bible to enable us to read Scripture well. This example shows us that we also need to be aware of our *own* history and culture when interpreting texts. We bring assumptions, prejudices, insights, and blind spots to our reading. The best interpretations will come as we grow in cultural awareness of both the Bible and of our own place and time.

> **♀ YOU ARE HERE**
>
> The First Stage: Informational Reading with Ingrid
> - Reading through Three Avenues
> - Side Trip 1: Maps and Seeing
> - Understanding Different Literary Genres
> - Side Trip 2: Reading in St. Petersburg (and Other Places)
> - **Avoiding Common Interpretive Mistakes**

Avoiding Common Interpretive Mistakes

It's nice on a road trip if one of your party has some general familiarity with where you're going. An adventure on the open road is great fun, but missing a major turn or hitting a pothole that results in a flat tire is not. We've now reached the third and final portion of the trip where Ingrid is behind the wheel. For our third informational skill we want to learn how to avoid some common interpretive mistakes. The point of this skill is not to rob us of the joy of the journey but rather to protect us from wrong turns and unnecessary repairs that will slow us down.

Because we care about hearing God's voice from the Bible (not making it mean whatever we want it to), we should take care to practice interpretation in the best way. Good *informational* reading is *careful*, giving focused attention and our best intellectual capacities to the task of understanding. There are common mistakes in interpretation that are easy to make and easy to correct. These mistakes can be organized under two headings: language errors and reasoning errors.[17]

Language Errors

God is a speaking God, and the Bible is a book of words. While there are other ways and experiences by which we may get glimpses of God—such as emotions, beauty in art and nature, mysterious and spiritual experiences—no form of revelation is more central than the words of Scripture.

But because we are limited and sinful creatures living in a fallen world, we will regularly encounter misunderstandings in communication. Sometimes we can easily misunderstand a good friend. If talking face to face to someone with whom we have much in common can result in misunderstanding, how much more challenging is it to read and understand a text written by someone from a different language, culture, place, and time? This may be especially true when we study the Bible because we try so hard to derive deeper meaning from it. Ironically, this expectation and respect for the Bible can lead us to treat its words in a magical way that results in more confusion than clarity, more error than truth.

For example, when studying Scripture we sometimes put too much emphasis on what a particular word *really* means by focusing on its origin and history—that is, its etymology—or on how we use the word in more technical contexts. Take the word *butterfly*, for example. Any speaker of English knows that, despite its constituent parts, this noun does not refer to a stick of churned milk soaring through the sky. *Butterfly* is an agreed upon set of sounds that points to a commonly known family of insects. We don't determine the meaning of the word through a dissection of its parts—*butter* and *fly*. Yet this kind of mistake is often foisted on words in the Bible. For example, the common Greek word *ekballō* comes from the preposition *ek* ("out of") and the verb *ballō* (often meaning "to throw"). Sometimes this word is used to mean to "cast or throw [something] out," like a group of demons in Matthew 8:31. But the same word can also be used with a less etymologically derived meaning of "bring out" such as in Matthew 12:35 where the good man and the bad man both "bring out" treasures good and bad—not "throw them out."

Similarly, we should always be careful to let the meaning of a word be determined by its use in its own context rather than assuming that the same word means the same thing everywhere. For example, the important biblical words for "righteous/righteousness" (Hebrew: *tsedaqah*; Greek: *dikaiosunē*) are rich and varied in meaning and usage. "Righteousness" in the Old Testament means primarily doing what is right according to God's commands, and this is its usage in the Gospel of Matthew as well. In Paul's writings it has slightly different but related senses of being declared in a right standing and of God's bringing justice or righteousness to the world. Matthew's use of "righteous" focuses more on the virtuous way of living that accords with God's coming kingdom than on a sense of things being put right in the world and with us. Matthew's and Paul's meanings are not contradictory, but neither are they the same. We will create a lot of confusion for ourselves and for others if we assume that *dikaiosunē* necessarily means exactly the same thing when different authors use it.

Many other examples of language errors could be identified, but we can sum up the point by emphasizing our need to pay close attention to what is communicated in Scripture and to use good *common sense*. We can avoid many language errors when we take care not to be overly technical in our arguments while at the same time not making too many assumptions about what an author is saying.

Reasoning Errors

Not only can we easily make mistakes with language but we also commonly commit errors in our logical reasoning. The effect of sin on our minds (see Rom. 1) means that logical arguments or patterns of reasoning can often appear sound when they are, in fact, not.

For example, consider the following argument:

All cats are hairy.
Rover the dog is hairy.
Therefore, Rover the dog is a cat.

While the absurd conclusion makes us realize that the argument is false, it may not be immediately clear to us *why* the argument is not only untrue but also poorly argued. This argument is invalid because although the first two statements are true, the relationship between them is not logically binding. That is, the assertion of the universal hairiness of cats does not mean that other animals, such as dogs, cannot also be hairy. Therefore, since the first statement does not necessarily relate to the second statement, the conclusion is invalid.

We often do the same thing when we are trying to understand a theological truth in a biblical passage. We often don't realize that our argument is following the same kind of illogical reasoning. In the case above we have a classic logical fallacy of association, whereby the combination of the first and second premises create a false sense of necessity in the conclusion. We can make the same error when interpreting the Bible. For example, consider the following reasoning:

The disciples in the Bible cast out demons.

We are also disciples.

Therefore, we cast out demons.

This argument may seem sound, but it fails in the same way as the argument above. I'm not saying that later Christians have not cast out demons (I am sure they have); nevertheless, the conclusion does not derive from the premises. Just because disciples in the Bible cast out demons and Christians today are also disciples, it does not logically follow that every disciple today casts out demons. This *could* happen, but it is not logically necessary because other factors may be at play—such as the unique status of Jesus's original disciples, special times when the gospel is advancing and is accompanied by miracles (as in Acts), and the fact that different people have different spiritual gifts (see 1 Cor. 12:4–11, 27–31).

In our study of the Bible we often commit these kinds of reasoning errors, especially when we want to assert something that we think is true and good. Such ways of arguing may win the day but will always prove to be foolish and damaging in the long run.

This warning to avoid common interpretive mistakes is an invitation to be *careful* in our arguments about what Holy Scripture is saying. As a result of our human limitations and the effects of sin, we do often make language and reasoning mistakes, so we should be humble and thoughtful in the task of interpreting the Bible.

The Second Stage of the Journey

Theological Reading with Tom

📍 **YOU ARE HERE**

The Second Stage: Theological Reading with Tom

- The Context of the Canon—Canonical Reading
- Side Trip 3: Our Right and Left Brains
- The Context of the Church's Tradition—Traditioned Reading
- Side Trip 4: Two T. Rexes and the Gestalt Shift
- The Context of Creedal Orthodoxy—Creedal Reading

During the first leg of our journey, Ingrid showed us the beauty and goodness of an informational reading—skills and knowledge that help us read well. No one would disagree that these approaches add value. But now it is time for another driver. Tom is happy to take his turn behind the wheel and provide us with another aspect of reading Scripture well—a *theological* reading.

ORIENTATION

The *theological* element of good reading encompasses several ideas. In the first instance it means that our interpretation must truly be concerned with God from beginning to end. The primary topic of Scripture is God himself. Thus, we don't just read to find historical information but to learn about God. The God of the Bible is triune—one God in three persons (Father, Son, and Spirit)—so a theological reading will necessarily be Trinitarian. Reading theologically also involves paying attention to the scope of the whole Bible, learning how the church before our time interpreted the biblical texts, and understanding how the church's creeds help us read.

Filling Up the Tank

Ingrid's informational reading taught us skills that will help us be better readers of *any* book, not just the Bible. This is an example of general hermeneutics. But to read the Bible well, we also need to develop skills that are more specific. While the Bible is a *human* book, written by human authors, bearing the marks of human culture and history, it is also *divine* revelation. Therefore, when we read and interpret Scripture we need more than a *general* hermeneutical understanding; we need a truly *theological* way of reading. A theological reading is not the opposite of the informational skills we learned from Ingrid. But it is founded on something deeper and goes beyond these techniques. All the informational techniques for reading well are helpful, but as one theologian points out, these skills "need to be *recontextualized* within a theological framework."[1] The Bible is a historical book, but it is more than that. Since the Bible is divine revelation, we need *theological* skills to read it well. We need Tom's theological focus to make our journey successful.

At the core of our word *theology* is God (Greek: *theos*). The God of the Bible is triune. He is one God in three persons: Father, Son, and Spirit. This means that we can and should read every text, including in the Old Testament, with the understanding that the eternal God has always been three persons. This is the foundation of a theological reading. With this Trinitarian foundation, a theological interpretation will also consciously read the texts of Scripture within three theological contexts that go beyond informational skills and techniques: the contexts of the canon (*canonical*), the church's tradition (*traditional*), and creedal orthodoxy (*creedal*).

YOU ARE HERE

The Second Stage: Theological Reading with Tom

- **The Context of the Canon—Canonical Reading**
- Side Trip 3: Our Right and Left Brains
- The Context of the Church's Tradition—Traditioned Reading
- Side Trip 4: Two T. Rexes and the Gestalt Shift
- The Context of Creedal Orthodoxy—Creedal Reading

The Context of the Canon—Canonical Reading

God has not only inspired individual writings and providentially preserved them for his church, but his Spirit has also led the church to recognize which writings are inspired and to put them together into a certain form and structure. We call this curated collection of writings the *canon* of Scripture. For the Christian this canon is twofold, consisting of what we now call the Old Testament (what the Jewish people of the first century simply called the Scriptures) and what we call the New Testament (the writings of the apostles and some of their associates).[2]

This collection of inspired writings spans more than two thousand years of different authors from different cultures writing in different languages, so it is inevitably varied and complex. But the formation of the canon presupposes that despite this diversity the *unified and singular* voice of God is woven throughout. Because God is one and is congruent in himself, his speaking through Scripture is ultimately consistent with itself. Amid the Bible's great and beautiful complexity is a profound singularity.

Thus when we are reading any part of Scripture, we must always remember that every text is part of something larger than itself—the inspired canon of Scripture. And this whole canon is ultimately consistent because it is all spoken by the one God. The theological unity of Scripture means that all of its texts fit together and speak in harmony—not in cacophony.

So if a text or idea in the Bible seems to be in tension with another text or idea, we must work at trying to understand how these diverse messages fit together. The Protestant Reformers addressed this canonical reality with the idea of the *analogy* of Scripture—that is, Scripture must be used to interpret other Scripture. For example, many biblical texts clearly speak about human responsibility and the moral culpability that comes with our choices to do right or wrong (see, e.g., Matt. 7:24–27; Eph. 5:1–21; Heb. 4:1–13). We are continually exhorted to seek the Lord, to do what is right, to love God and others, and to repent of sin. Yet at the same time, other texts of Scripture teach plainly that we can do no ultimate good apart from the power of God's Spirit making us born again (a passive metaphor), causing us to see, and enabling us to walk in righteousness. We are clay molded by God the potter for his own purposes (see, e.g., John 6:44; Rom. 5:5–11; 9:10–21).

The Bible's canonical whole invites us to work diligently to understand how both of these truths can be affirmed at the same time. Quite often the answer will lie in recognizing the mystery and paradoxical truths of who God is. That's a good thing and appropriate for us as creatures who are limited in our ability to understand God. But we start and end with the presupposition that the canon is consistent within itself. From this theological commitment we work toward understanding. The alternative to this theological position results in paralysis. If there is no ultimate unity in Scripture, then there is no way to adjudicate the diverse voices within Scripture. The result is a complete lack of scriptural authority.

Canonical reading also helps us read the Bible with categories we call *redemptive history* or *biblical theology*. A redemptive historical or biblical theological reading of Scripture sees the Bible as a whole story, tracing ideas and themes that go beyond the individual books. This is different than *systematic theology*, which is a topical gathering together and organizing (systematically) of the teachings of Scripture on different matters such as the nature of God, salvation, and the final state of humans. Redemptive historical / biblical theological approaches are not in conflict with systematic theology but are distinct and complementary.

So, for example, the theme of God's presence can be traced across books as diverse as Genesis, Ezekiel, Matthew, John, 1 Thessalonians, and Revelation. We can pull on threads of this theme that pop up from the garden of Eden to the new creation. By doing so we begin to see a pattern in the tapestry of Scripture that is bigger than the individual books. This canonical reading reveals patterns God has put into the world and into Scripture that are only discernible when you pull up high enough to look at the whole. There are countless other theological topics that can be traced across the canon in this way, such as the Messiah, the day of the Lord, the kingdom of God, and creation / new creation.

Additionally, we can recognize that not only are certain themes repeated throughout the Bible but also that a discernible story drives the whole. The biblical canon is not a collection of inspired but random spiritual perspectives. Rather, the canon presents a unified story that is spiritual and historical—God is acting in history to do good to the world and to the people he has made. Thus, whenever reading any part of the Bible, we ought to ask where this particular text fits into the overall story that runs from creation to new creation.

Yet another way a canon consciousness benefits our reading of the Bible is that we can learn to read *figurally*. This means learning to hear resonances and see connections across the canon. Certain ideas recur and build on one another as the canon unfolds.

For example, many stories in the Bible encourage us to see figural connections between various wilderness feedings, miraculous water crossings, mountaintop revelations of God, and connections of the numbers three, ten, twelve, forty, and seventy. It is no mere coincidence that God's people cross bodies of water in miraculous ways: the Red Sea at the exodus (Exod. 14.21–22), the Jordan River as Israel enters the promised land (Josh. 4:1–18; 2 Kings 2:8), and ultimately, the Sea of Galilee when Jesus reveals himself to his disciples (Matt. 14:23–27). In each case some new work of God is happening—confirmed by a demonstration of his power over creation. Then, in the final state of the new creation, there is no longer a sea (Rev. 21:1). In Scripture bodies of water, and the monstrous creatures they harbor, often serve as metaphors for forces of chaos (e.g., Gen. 1:2; Job 41:1–34; Pss. 69:1–2; 73:13). Thus, in the end, all chaos is calmed and conquered finally because God himself is present (Rev. 21:2–3). This is just one example of thousands of ways in which the canon contains figurations—recurring, multi-directional connections that enrich our understanding. Although the many skills and techniques developed in an informational reading are helpful, they cannot provide the whole-Bible insights that a canonical reading can.

TAKE A TURN AT THE WHEEL

One of the many themes or patterns we can see throughout Scripture is the temple—the place where God meets with humanity.

Trace the theme of the temple throughout the Bible. All the while, ask how different stages contribute to our understanding of what it means for God to dwell with humans. What changes occur in the temple idea as we progress through the Bible?

Here are a few texts to consider (there are many more!): 1 Kings 8; Isaiah 66:1–2; John 1:14; John 4:19–26; 1 Corinthians 3:16–17; Revelation 11:1–19.

You can also get help from some teachers who have written on this theme.[3]

YOU ARE HERE

The Second Stage: Theological Reading with Tom
- The Context of the Canon—Canonical Reading
- **Side Trip 3: Our Right and Left Brains**
- The Context of the Church's Tradition—Traditioned Reading
- Side Trip 4: Two T. Rexes and the Gestalt Shift
- The Context of Creedal Orthodoxy—Creedal Reading

Side Trip 3: Our Right and Left Brains

For well over a hundred years, neurologists and psychologists have been trying to figure out how the various parts of our brains work. Experiments and studies have revealed many insights about how particular sections of our brains control specific functions like speech, smell, sight, emotions, movement, and fight-or-flight responses. Researchers have especially learned from stroke victims and those who have received injuries to localized parts of the brain. In these cases, impaired functions can be tied directly to physical brain locations.

But this intriguing data doesn't explain everything. And often the data is confusing. The brain (let alone the mind) is incredibly complex. Scientists need more than data. They also need theories to organize and make sense of the observed phenomena.

This means that different theories come and go, each of which explains some of the complex data while ignoring others. Over time many theories are proven to be mistaken. Further research combined with a better theoretical explanation often replaces inferior ways of understanding.

In recent years one such widespread but mistaken theory of the brain is being radically overturned. The old idea was that the left and right hemispheres of our brains control completely different functions. In its popularized version this became the pervasive assumption that people can be classified as either "right brain people" (creative) or "left brain people" (logical, analytical). This common notion has no basis in neurology or psychology, and it is demonstrably false.

As a result, most researchers have long abandoned trying to figure out what the difference is between the two sides of our brains. Everyone agrees that there are differences—size, shape, and some functions. But no theory has been able to make sense of the wide range of data. That is, until the pioneering and magisterial work of Dr. Iain McGilchrist.

McGilchrist is a rare bird who was educated in English literature at Oxford and then went back to school to become a psychiatric doctor specializing in neuroimaging and therapy. He has been a leader in this field of medicine. His breadth of learning in history, literature, philosophy, and neuroscience is on full display in his field-shattering book, *The Master and His Emissary: The Divided Brain and the Making of the Western World*.[4]

Through a thorough review of neurological data and a keen idea for how things connect together, McGilchrist revisits the brain hemisphere debate and offers a comprehensive theory that finally explains this confusing aspect of brain science. He argues that the differences in our brain hemispheres do not make us logical or creative personality types but instead affect *the kind of attention we give to the world*. In all people the two hemispheres of our brains attend to the world in different ways: the left brain focuses on analysis and details while the right brain makes sense of the whole, creating a picture of understanding. These two different types of attention are both necessary for humans (and countless other animals) to function in the world.

McGilchrist gives many examples from neurology, psychology, and history to show how his theory comprehensively explains our human existence in how we relate to the world around us. But he doesn't stop there. One big goal of *The Master and His Emissary* is hinted at in the subtitle. McGilchrist argues convincingly that something bad has happened in the modern Western world, namely, that we have inverted the values of what our two hemispheres do for the human. The "master" who sees all, makes sense of the whole, and therefore can guide us well is the right brain. The "emissary"—the left brain—is the analytical bureaucrat who plays an essential but limited role. But the problem in the modern Western world is that we have come to value the left brain's role over the right brain's. The emissary has risen up and taken over from the master. We have exalted science (largely a left brain-driven activity) as the true way of knowing. The result is a very reductionistic and non-holistic way of understanding the world and humanity.

Much more can be said about McGilchrist's argument and its implications. But how does this relate to our goal of reading the Bible well? In many ways, McGilchrist's insight is underneath the whole approach of this book with its threefold mode of reading. Ingrid is a left-brainer in the sense that what she emphasizes is the analytic. This is good and necessary for our journey of interpretation. But it's not enough. To function well we also need right-brain activities—putting information into a coherent whole, making sense of things by seeing how the parts fit into a bigger picture. Our other two friends on the journey, Tom and Taylor, will provide much of this right brain function to supplement Ingrid's helpful tools. The reason I have written this book is because, in line with McGilchrist's critique of the modern Western world, we have often reduced biblical interpretation to the informational skills without integrating these into a holistic approach to reading the Bible well.

> **YOU ARE HERE**
>
> The Second Stage: Theological Reading with Tom
>
> - The Context of the Canon—Canonical Reading
> - Side Trip 3: Our Right and Left Brains
> - **The Context of the Church's Tradition—Traditioned Reading**
> - Side Trip 4: Two T. Rexes and the Gestalt Shift
> - The Context of Creedal Orthodoxy—Creedal Reading

The Context of the Church's Tradition—Traditioned Reading

The second way in which we can engage in a theological reading is by listening to the voices of those who have gone before us when reading the same texts of Scripture. We call this simply the tradition of the church. A traditional reading, or better, *traditioned*—that is, trained or conditioned by the tradition—reading of the Scriptures involves listening to and looking over the shoulders of skilled theologians of the church. This includes scholars and pastors who approach the Bible with a set of important questions about theology: Who is God? What is he like? How does he operate? What is he doing in the world? Where do we fit in?

For some Christians *tradition* sounds scary and suspicious. But the Bible itself recognizes the importance of tradition. Throughout the Old Testament, God's people are reminded to pass on to their children what they have learned (e.g., Deut. 6:1–9). In the New Testament Paul challenges the believers in Thessalonica not to stray from the traditions they had been taught concerning Jesus (2 Thess. 2:15; 3:6), and he commends the Corinthians to hold fast to the traditions he taught them (1 Cor. 11:2). At times traditions can be ungodly and can prevent people from hearing Scripture correctly (see, e.g., Matt. 15:1–11), but this is not normally the case. Traditions are good in shaping and guiding God's people.

Moreover, everyone is influenced by traditions whether they realize it or not. All of us have had our presuppositions, sensibilities, and convictions trained in some context, and this affects us deeply in ways both conscious and subconscious.[5] No one is free from traditions, nor should we be. Traditions contain hard-wrought wisdom that serves us for the good. The great composer Gustav Mahler is reported to have said it this way: "Tradition is not the worship of ashes but the preservation of fire."[6] We can think of this kind of traditioned reading in two aspects—systematic theology and the history of interpretation.

Systematic Theology

As the Christian faith spread geographically beyond the confines of Palestine and chronologically beyond the first century AD, it encountered reception, opposition, and corruption. That is, thousands of people found new life through the preached message of Christ while many others, both Jews and Gentiles, opposed the faith vehemently. At the same time, as always happens with ideas and beliefs, some people misunderstood it, misapplied it, and contorted its teachings into something different. As a result of all three of these responses to the faith, later Christians saw the need to write books explaining the proper interpretation and applications of biblical teaching. This started with commentaries and sermons from church leaders that explained the Scriptures correctly from a Christian perspective.[7]

But soon there was also a need to explain how all of the Bible and its teachings fit together as additional questions were raised concerning God, human nature, morality, salvation, the nature of Scripture, and the final state of the world. This is what we call theology, or in today's terminology, *systematic theology*. The "systematic" in systematic theology refers to the organization of the material into topics and categories to make it accessible. We now have 1,800 or so years' worth of people writing theology books. Sometimes theologians write on one aspect of theology, like the Trinity or the nature of salvation, and sometimes they produce multivolume works that seek to explain all aspects of theological study in a comprehensive way.

We can also think of systematic theology in terms of a holy imagination. That is, when we read the Bible closely and exegetically (like Ingrid emphasized) we engage in a kind of analytic reasoning. We break things down into their constituent parts so that we can examine and understand the bits. This is good and beneficial as far as it goes. But we also need to understand the whole. Theology uses our God-given imaginative, synthetic capabilities to bring together various biblical, philosophical, scientific, and experiential insights to make sense of the whole. (Recall the left and right brain hemispheres from the McGilchrist discussion above.) Theologian Kevin Vanhoozer observes that imagination enables us to discern fittingness "the way the parts belong to the whole." Theological imagination is a way of seeing how God's teachings and God's world fit together. "As such, the imagination is an essential ingredient in achieving biblical literacy, namely, the ability to see the various parts of a single, unified, and meaningful whole."[8]

But how does systematic theology relate to reading the Bible well? The answer lies in understanding that the Bible and theology, when properly read, have the same goal—the formation of humans into the image of Christ. The message of the gospel is not merely that God has come down to save sinners and take them to heaven (although that is true as far as it goes) but that God has come down to redeem creation itself and especially humans, reshaping them into the restored and glorified image of God through Christ by the power of the Spirit (see Rom. 8:18–30; 2 Cor. 3:18). That's a big sentence worth going back and rereading! The Bible and theology are given as gifts to the church to be used toward this end, to teach us the story of redemption and to call us to enter into that story. God is creating a holy nation, a kingdom of priests who will know him and glorify him (1 Pet. 2:9).

Vanhoozer describes it this way: "Theology serves the church by helping to shape its collective imagination so that its image of its body life, and everything else, is governed by the gospel message at the heart of the master story that unifies Scripture."[9] This is not saying that theology and the Bible are equal in their shaping value. Good theology is an explanation of biblical teaching, not a competitor. It is the Bible's teachings and story that shape our hearts, minds, and habits in the church. But systematic theology serves to organize, explain, and apply these teachings. As Vanhoozer notes, "Doctrine does not add content to Scripture, but it does add understanding."[10]

As an example, let's consider what theologians say about the biblical idea of the *imago Dei*, the image of God.[11] The idea that humans are made in the image of God is foundational to the biblical story. We read in Genesis that the invisible God imaged himself in the creation of humankind:

> So God created man in his own image,
>   in the image of God he created him;
>   male and female he created them. (Gen 1:27)

This becomes a fundamental idea in Jewish thinking and then even more so in Christian theology, with several New Testament texts employing this notion.[12]

But what exactly does it mean for humans to be made in God's image, especially when the Bible emphasizes that God is a spirit who is invisible and does not have a body like humans do (John 4:24; Col. 1:15; 1 Tim. 1:17)? Theologians over the centuries have debated this question and have given us a variety of theologically reasoned answers.

The most common understanding throughout history has been that the image of God refers to some capacity that humans share with God, such as our capacity for rational thought. This is what particularly distinguishes humans from the animals. More recent theologians have emphasized instead that the *imago Dei* is not so much about what humans *are* but what we *do*, our function in creation. Based on comparisons with other ancient Near Eastern cultures that also used the idea of the divine image, these theologians argue that humans are imaging God in our calling to rule over and tend creation; humans are vice-regents placed in God's royal garden. Yet other theologians instead have argued that the image of God refers to humanity's relational nature. Like God himself, humans are fundamentally relational—as male and female in relationship to each other, in relationship to God, and in relationship to creation. Finally, some theologians think a multifaceted approach that includes all three of these perspectives is necessary for a proper understanding of what it means to be made in the image of God.

Each of these theological approaches is based on Scripture's teachings. But the mere presence of verses that reference the image of God is not sufficient to explain fully what this concept means or its many implications. We need to read these verses closely, understand them in their various contexts, connect them to related ideas throughout the Bible, and then make judgments about how everything fits together. We need theologians to do this work, which includes studying the arguments of earlier theologians and dialoguing with their views to discern what is helpful and what is not. Not every Christian is capable of or called to this kind of study, but the church needs theologians to engage in this work and to communicate their understanding to help us make the best sense of what the Bible is teaching.

The History of Interpretation

We talked about the history of interpretation earlier when Ingrid was driving as part of the in-front-of-the-text reading skill. Now we're thinking about it more theologically—how we can learn from the tradition of Christians who have gone before us.

Simply put, the best reading of Scripture will listen to the tradition of how faithful Christians have interpreted the text—especially wise and gifted leaders—throughout the history of the church. There is no virtue in trying to understand the Bible apart from the riches of the tradition of other readers from the church's past.

Let's look at an example to see how this kind of reading works out. In Matthew, Mark, and Luke, we find the famous story about Jesus being revealed in his glory to three of his disciples on a mountain shortly before he enters Jerusalem for the last time (see Matt. 17:1–8; Mark 9:2–8; Luke 9:28–36). We call this story the transfiguration, referring to Jesus's appearance being transformed from lowly peasant to glorious Lord. Jesus's clothing becomes dazzlingly white, his face shines, and he is accompanied by Moses and Elijah, who are discussing the things of God with him. The scene is so stunning and unexpected for the disciples that, in a semi-coherent stupor, Peter suggests that they build three little tabernacles and stay there forever.

This is a rich story that communicates many big theological truths. Today, most interpreters emphasize that this story teaches us about Jesus's unity with God; he is revealed as glorious like God is. This is a glimpse of his true divine identity that will be known only fully after his death and resurrection. Commentators also often observe that this revealing of Jesus's glorious nature is intentionally framed on either side with references to his forthcoming suffering and death. This reinforces the Christian paradox of the way of the cross—life and flourishing come through suffering.

Interestingly, while not denying these insights, throughout most of the church's history, the transfiguration has been read very differently. Traditionally, this story has been interpreted in two main ways. First, earlier interpreters often emphasized that Peter's words to Jesus were another example of his misunderstanding of Jesus's mission and his foolish attempt to redirect Jesus's plans. Right before this story, after Peter's confession at Caesarea Philippi, Jesus told his disciples that he was going to suffer and die, and Peter tried to correct him, receiving a strong rebuke from his Lord (Matt. 16:13–27). Many interpreters see the same thing happening at the transfiguration. Peter's suggestion that they stay on the mountain to build tabernacles is another example of his misunderstanding of Jesus's true mission.

Even more interesting and significant than this, the primary way the transfiguration story was interpreted historically was in connection with the beatific vision. The beatific vision was a major theological idea throughout most of the church's history and remains so especially in the traditions other than Protestantism. The beatific vision refers to the Christian hope that true happiness

(Latin: *beatus*) will be achieved when we see God. The end goal of the Christian faith is not eternal rounds of perfect golf in heaven but is instead what will make humans truly happy—seeing the triune God as he is in all his beauty and glory. When this goal becomes the reality, then and only then can a human enter into full shalom and flourishing. This is the point of the transfiguration story. Jesus's glorious appearance is a foretaste of this hope, with Jesus as the face of God now revealed to humanity. However, because this theological idea has been largely lost within the Protestant tradition,[13] many modern interpreters no longer understand the transfiguration story this way. You have to study the history of interpretation to run into this beatific vision reading.

In light of this, we can make a couple of important observations about reading with the history of interpretation. On the one hand, changes in theological understanding across time affect what people see in the biblical text. Biblical interpretation is influenced by theological commitments (see more on this below). At the same time, when we study the history of the interpretation of a biblical text we learn other ways of reading the text, insights that may have been lost and theological truths that are worth recovering. Good reading will seek to understand the ways that the church in the past has read the text differently than we do, thus enriching our understanding.

Thus, at the practical level this aspect of theological reading means that when we read Scripture we listen to the voice of other speakers in the history of interpretation, especially those who come from traditions other than our own and who help us see some of our own blind spots. If we want to be serious students of Scripture, we will read and study, with an open heart and mind, what others have to say. Thankfully, there are massive resources available to us from the history of tradition. Smart and godly people have been studying the Bible for a long time! Today one can easily find access to commentaries and sermons from a wide variety of interpreters who have gone before us: from Origen to Augustine to John Calvin to Jonathan Edwards to Charles Spurgeon.

TAKE A TURN AT THE WHEEL

When Ingrid was driving we talked about *Wirkungsgeschichte* and reception history. Many of the same resources mentioned above are helpful when we think about the history of interpretation. David Paul Parris's *Reading the Bible with Giants*,[14] the Ancient Christian Commentary on Scripture series by InterVarsity Press, and the Christian Classics Ethereal Library (ccel.org) are all helpful in accessing earlier interpretations. But these only scratch the surface of the great mass of sources available to us.

To try your hand at this fascinating way of reading, take one of Jesus's Beatitudes (Matt. 5:3–12), such as Matthew 5:5: "Blessed are the meek, for they shall inherit the earth." Using print or online resources, make a chart summarizing how the following interpreters read this text: Augustine, Jerome, Martin Luther, John Calvin, Jonathan Edwards, Charles Spurgeon, and John Wesley. What similarities are there? What differences? Which readings do you find most helpful? Afterwards, if you want to dig deeper, check out chapter 5 of Rebekah Eklund's excellent book, *The Beatitudes through the Ages*.[15]

YOU ARE HERE

The Second Stage: Theological Reading with Tom
- The Context of the Canon—Canonical Reading
- Side Trip 3: Our Right and Left Brains
- The Context of the Church's Tradition—Traditioned Reading
- **Side Trip 4: Two T. Rexes and the Gestalt Shift**
- The Context of Creedal Orthodoxy—Creedal Reading

Side Trip 4: Two T. Rexes and the Gestalt Shift

The run-up to Christmas in my city, like most places in the US, witnesses a wide variety of yard adornments celebrating the season. Some are gaudy inflatables of Christmas cartoony creatures. Some are simply glowing messages of "Peace" or "Seasons Greetings" (absent the needed apostrophe). And many are, appropriately, scenes representing the real "reason for the season"—the nativity scene. The holy family, angels, shepherds, animals, and wise men (who according to the biblical text didn't arrive for a couple of years, but that's OK) compose a popular form of front lawn festive images.

When I was growing up, nativity scenes came in two versions: (1) temporary live ones, sponsored by a church with people dressed up to reenact the first Christmas, and (2) scenes with painted statues. I'm not sure when the transition occurred, but today during Christmas I rarely see either of those versions. Instead, the most common form of the nativity scene I encounter now is the white, wooden cut out style. They are usually about 4 feet tall and provide stylized silhouettes of Mary, Joseph, and a few animals. This representation is fine enough. It gets the basic idea across, even including a healthy dash of piety with Mary and Joseph in prayerful positions and a halo indicating baby Jesus's divine status.

But what the original makers of this now-popular version did not anticipate is that if you look at this scene in a different way, it communicates something absurdly funny. Mary and Joseph's prayer postures look strikingly like tyrannosaurus rexes rearing their heads while the halo on the baby crib between them looks like a table saw in action. We could put a label across the bottom of this picture that reads, "Two T. Rexes Fighting Over a Table Saw." And once you do that, there's no going back. Once you see it, you can't unsee it.[16]

This change in perspective on what we are seeing is called a "Gestalt shift." The German word *Gestalt* means "form," and when used to describe the psychological experience of seeing something in a different way, the word means "a pattern or configuration." Gestalt psychology arose in the early twentieth century as a different way of thinking about the human experience. Particularly, Gestalt theorists argued that the whole is more than the sum of its parts and that humans experience the world not through atomistic elements but as a whole. It is the whole that makes sense of the parts, not the other way around. So when we look at the nativity scene, the elemental parts don't change, but suddenly we can come to see the whole differently: not a pious scene in a barn but an absurd and unexpected image of fighting dinosaurs. The actual picture has not changed. Rather, we come to perceive the whole scene differently. And once the whole is perceived differently, the parts take on different meaning.

The same thing can happen with another nativity scene, this one from a postage stamp. A well-meaning UK Royal Mail stamp from 2015 depicted Mary and Joseph from afar against a starry night.[17]

At some point in the world of online memes, it was noted that it looks like Mary is playing keyboard and Joseph singing vocals. The raised crib looks like a keyboard stand and Joseph's staff becomes a mic stand and mic. Once again, this is a Gestalt shift—another holistic way of seeing the parts. And in both of these cases, the power of the Gestalt shift is the absurdity of the juxtaposition of the one way of seeing with the other.

In the latter part of the twentieth century, these notions resurfaced in a different form in the world of cognitive linguistics. In cognitive linguistics scholars talk about construals and frames. Construals and frames are ways of seeing. The world is full of innumerable data points—more than any human brain can interpret at once. So how we make sense of the world is through a construal or frame that organizes, highlights, deselects, and creates correspondences and causal relations among the data. The construal is a Gestalt, a shape or form that gives us a sense of the whole rather than just the parts. And one of the most powerful human experiences is when one construal is replaced with another, when a shift in the Gestalt happens and we come to see in a different way. Philosophers of language have even described this eye-opening experience as a conversion—a new way of seeing what was there all along.

This can happen to us when we read the Bible as well. For example, if you've never thought about the message of the gospel in terms of God's restoring his kingdom on the earth, there are a lot of things in the Gospels that you may ignore. But once you start to think of Jesus's message and work as bringing God's kingdom into the world—that this is the "good news"—then all of a sudden so much makes sense. The Gestalt shift happens, and the message of the New Testament starts to fit together more fully. The gospel of the kingdom is why Jesus calls people to repent, because a new reign with a new King (Jesus) is arriving on the earth (Matt. 4:17). This also clarifies why it is so important that Jesus is the Son of David, because he must be the rightful King who also fulfills the promise that a descendant of David would once again reign on his throne. Additionally, this is why so many of Jesus's parables use royal scenes and have characters such as kings, princes, and landowners who have servants.

The Gestalt shift toward understanding the gospel as being about the kingdom also explains why the message of "eternal life" in the Gospel of John at first appears to be so different from the message of the coming kingdom in Matthew, Mark, and Luke. From an ancient Jewish perspective the "eternal life" that they were looking forward to referred to the time and space when God would return as King to establish his reign and to bring shalom upon the earth. To receive or inherit or enter into eternal life meant to enter into God's kingdom where the true flourishing or shalom life could be found. The "eternal life" that Jesus talks about in John is not some disembodied existence in heaven; it is nothing other than the life of God's people lived together in a renewed earth with God reigning as king—that is, the kingdom of God.

This is just one example of how seeing the Bible with a new (biblically rooted) Gestalt enables us to see the parts differently and make more sense of them. This also happens when we read the Bible with the help of the orthodox creeds and confessions. Key framing truths from the creeds about the triune nature of God, the two natures of Christ united in one man, the future hope of the bodily resurrection, and so on, enable us to see how the various teachings of Scripture fit together and make more sense when seen from the perspective of the whole.

YOU ARE HERE

The Second Stage: Theological Reading with Tom

- The Context of the Canon—Canonical Reading
- Side Trip 3: Our Right and Left Brains
- The Context of the Church's Tradition—Traditioned Reading
- Side Trip 4: Two T. Rexes and the Gestalt Shift
- **The Context of Creedal Orthodoxy—Creedal Reading**

The Context of Creedal Orthodoxy—Creedal Reading

So far we have seen that the contexts of canon and tradition play an important role in interpreting the Bible well. But there is one more theological context to consider: the context of the church's orthodox creeds. The word creed comes from the Latin verb *credo*, meaning "I believe." The creeds are the personal and communal statements of what Christians openly confess as their belief.

In the first several centuries of Christianity, orthodox believers wrestled with the best way to articulate the teachings of Scripture and the reality of Jesus Christ. These articulations were codified in the church's great creeds such as the Apostles' Creed and the Nicene Creed. These creeds are not Scripture, but they do reflect the true church's understanding of what the Bible says in light of various challenges and misunderstandings that arose in the early church. Later in church history, longer documents were written called confessions—confessing the beliefs of particular Christian groups. These were especially prevalent at times when there was a need to revive and clarify the teachings of the Bible, such as during the Protestant Reformation in the sixteenth century.[18]

Theologian J. V. Fesko identifies three important functions that creeds play in the church—to serve as boundary markers that distinguish orthodoxy from heterodoxy, to create room for differences of opinion within the circle of orthodoxy, and to connect the church to its historical past.[19]

We call the teachings of the creeds and confessions *doctrines.* Alister McGrath defines doctrines as the "communally authoritative teachings regarded as essential to the identity of the Christian community."[20] Doctrines do not replace Scripture, but they are essential to the formation and guidance of the church. Even as we have a canon of writings we call Scripture, so too we have a set of beliefs that are essential to a right understanding of the Christian faith.

Not all doctrines are equally important. Many doctrines have different interpretations even within the orthodox church, such as mode of baptism (infant or believer). But the big doctrines, the ones that define the boundaries of the Christian community, are recorded in the conciliar creeds (such as the Nicene Creed and the Chalcedonian Definition). These are the creeds and doctrines that all three major branches of orthodox Christianity (Roman Catholic, Eastern Orthodox, Protestant) affirm. The conciliar creeds are foundational truths that span all the centuries and breadth of Christianity.

It took a few centuries for these creeds to be firmly established and clarified. But even before the various creeds were solidified, Christians understood that the tradition of the apostles' teaching was continuing (cf. 1 Cor. 11:2; 2 Thess. 2:15; 3:6). This handed-down tradition of true teaching was described as the *regula fidei* or "rule of faith" by the church fathers.[21] The "rule" here means something like what we mean when we refer to a "rule of thumb"—a measurement that points to the center and boundaries of the right reading of Scripture.[22] The rule of faith is the theological framework in which Christians have always understood the complexity of the Bible's teachings. It is "a distillation of core Christian teaching that can help unveil the inherent patterns of Scripture"[23] and the basic summary of the Christian faith.

As noted, there are differences of opinion on many issues within the circle of orthodoxy. The oldest conciliar creeds (or what we can call the essential rule of faith) focus on the highest level doctrinal issues—the nature of God as triune (including how Jesus as the incarnate Son of God is simultaneously God and human), God's relationship to the world in saving and redeeming us by his grace, and the future state of the world in God's sovereign plan. Beyond these essentials, many Christians have written more specific confessions to distinguish their understanding of biblical teaching from other groups within the faith.

The point of all this is to say that a good reading of the Bible will be done within the context of the rule of faith. For some modern Christians, however, this seems problematic. Many Christians in recent centuries have been taught that they don't need theology, only the Bible. Some have rallied around the cry, "No creed but Jesus." They claim we simply need to pursue the original meaning of the biblical text by utilizing our informational techniques and skills.

This sounds very noble. But attempting to read Scripture apart from the context of creedal orthodox doctrine is both impossible and unwise. It is impossible because there is no theology-free zone in which we can do our thinking. Our values, judgments, and affections all depend on some belief system.[24]

It is unwise because we need the wisdom of others to guide and protect our thinking.

This is what the Protestant Reformers said. Martin Luther, John Calvin, Ulrich Zwingli, and others strongly fought against many of the Roman Catholic Church's traditions in their day because they believed that these later traditions were not rightly based on the Bible. They did so under the banner of *sola scriptura* ("Scripture alone"). But it is clear that the Reformers *never meant by this that we are neutral readers or that we should read the Bible apart from creedal orthodoxy.* Rather, they meant that Scripture alone is *the ultimate authority* and the revelation upon which all doctrine is built. This is the same thing that the creators of the creeds argued. The "alone" (*sola*) of this Protestant principle refers to what alone is the ultimate authority—Scripture. The "alone" is not saying that *only* Scripture matters. The "alone" is not denying the importance of establishing creeds and doctrines. After all, God has given to the church the ongoing role of teachers and preachers to guide our understanding of what the Bible teaches. Listening to preachers and teachers (and reading books like this one) are part of the *sola scriptura* principle. Everything taught and written must ultimately be submitted to God's Word, but we don't *only* read the Bible on our own.

The creeds are not in competition with the Bible. The creeds help and serve believers. We made the same observation above when discussing systematic theology. It is worth quoting Kevin Vanhoozer on this point again: "Theology [and, we could say, creedal orthodoxy] serves the church by helping to shape its collective imagination so that its image of its body life, and everything else, is governed by the gospel message at the heart of the master story that unifies Scripture."[25] In other words, the creeds, rooted in Scripture, give us a frame and guidance for how to understand who God is and who we are.

The creeds and the rule of faith are necessary for a good *theological* reading because having the Scriptures alone—even with an agreed-upon canon—does not mean that we will be able to understand God's message rightly. Even when we use the same techniques, people end up with radically different interpretations of the Bible. After all, most cults and heresies, both in ancient times and today, use the same Bible that orthodox believers do and usually with the same tools of study. Yet their readings are not the same.

As an example, let's consider for a moment the various groups within Judaism in Jesus's day. The Pharisees, Sadducees, and Essenes in the first century all revered God's word. Yet they understood the meaning of these texts very differently. Their differences cannot be explained on the basis of a greater set of exegetical skills or belief in the historical veracity of the texts.[26] Rather, each of these groups had different theological commitments and beliefs. Of the many different ways that Scripture can be read, each community understood the texts in light of their overarching belief system. The Jewish people at Qumran read their Bible very differently than those in Jerusalem and Samaria, based on other commitments and teachings.

So too with the earliest (Jewish) Christians. They believed in the same Jewish Scriptures as the Pharisees did, and they read with the same skills and methods. But Christians read the Pentateuch, Psalms, and Prophets differently—in a new way centered on Jesus. They reread the Jewish Scriptures anew in light of the incarnation, life, death, resurrection, and ascension of Jesus whom they believed to be the Messiah sent by God.

As Joel Green observes,

> What makes a "Christian reading" of Israel's Scriptures (rather
> than, say, a Pharisaic or Essene reading of those same Scriptures)
> are especially those theological lenses by which the followers of
> Christ have identified the God of Abraham, Isaac, and Jacob
> with the God who raised Jesus from the dead.[27]

So we see that just having the Bible does not guarantee that the
Bible will be read well. Even an agreed-upon set of methods is not
enough. Theological commitments—doctrinal creeds—help us
read the Bible faithfully.

The church fathers understood this in their own struggles with
sundry heresies that spun away from the Christian church. Irenaeus
famously spoke about the rule of faith as the guiding principle
that enables us to put together the many pieces of Scripture into
the right overall picture. He points out that orthodox Christians
and heretical groups like the Gnostics are both reading the same
Scriptures and exegeting the same texts. But despite this they end
up with different pictures of who Jesus is: for the Christians he is
the Davidic King; for the Gnostics he is but a dog or fox.[28] It's like
having a pile of colored mosaic tiles. Both Christians and Gnostics
have the same pile of tiles, but they create different pictures from
them. The differences between their pictures are not the tiles themselves but the overall picture they make, the picture that represents
reality. The Christian reader of the Bible is guided by what is really
true, as helpfully articulated in the rule of faith. The rule of faith
does not control the Scriptures, but rather it serves as a map with
boundaries and a center, a map that guides us on our joyful journey
of discovering the manifold riches of Scripture.[29]

TAKE A TURN AT THE WHEEL

One of the earliest and most foundational of the Christian confessions is called the Apostles' Creed. While it was not written by the apostles themselves, the church recognized that this confession does a good job summing up the apostolic teaching of the New Testament. Here is an English translation of this ancient creed:

I believe in God the Father Almighty,
    Maker of heaven and earth.

I believe in Jesus Christ, his only-begotten Son, our Lord;
    who was conceived by the Holy Spirit, born of the
        virgin Mary;
    suffered under Pontius Pilate;
    was crucified, dead, and buried;
    he descended into hell;
    the third day he rose again from the dead;
    he ascended into heaven;
    and sits at the right hand of God the Father
        Almighty;
    from there he shall come to judge the living and
        the dead.

I believe in the Holy Spirit;
    the holy catholic church;
    the communion of saints;

the forgiveness of sins;
the resurrection of the body;
and the life everlasting. Amen.[30]

Notice the moves of the creed. It has three parts that recognize the three persons of the Trinity. Notice that all three persons are the object of confessing belief, distinct but equal. Observe also that the creed encompasses the past, present, and future: it starts with creation, focuses on the historical and spiritual life of Jesus, acknowledges the ongoing experience of Christ's church, and looks forward to his future return. Note that the story of Jesus has several crucial parts: his conception, incarnation, suffering, death, resurrection, and ascension. These observations shape our reading of the New Testament, help us see the contours and emphases of what the New Testament authors are saying, and aid in organizing our thoughts and guiding our own interpretive moves.

Summary

These three contexts of a theological reading of Scripture—canonical, traditioned, and creedal—all speak with one voice to a Christological and Trinitarian reading of Scripture. Because God is one and because he has now ultimately spoken through his Son (Heb. 1:1), all Scripture ultimately speaks about Jesus the Son with a unified voice. This does not mean that every verse directly speaks about Jesus. But it does mean that a truly theological reading will be a reading of all the Scriptures (including the Old Testament) as pertaining to, witnessing to, and pointing to who God is for us in Christ. "For all the promises of God find their Yes in him. That is why it is through him that we utter our Amen to God for his glory" (2 Cor. 1:20). All the things that happened in Israel's history were written for Christians' instruction because we are the ones "on whom the end of the ages has come" (1 Cor. 10:11). This is what we call a Christological reading of the Bible.

And at the same time, a theological reading of Scripture can never be less than fully Trinitarian. Along with God the Father revealing himself through the Son, the Holy Spirit is fully present and at work. It is the Spirit of God who is guiding, empowering, and speaking. It is the Spirit of God who fills Jesus and guides him through the mysterious workings of the Trinity's interrelationships. And it is the Spirit who continues to mediate God's presence to the world through the church now that the Son has ascended to his heavenly throne. The Spirit also instructs and guides the church and its participants in our understanding of God's Holy Word.

Thus, once again, we need Tom on the trip with us to help us with a theological reading. Tom will constantly be reminding us that any time we are reading the Bible, the text we are studying is part of a large, complicated, beautiful, and unified canon of Scripture. Tom will also point us to Christians who have gone before us who have wrestled with the same texts in light of big theological ideas. Tom will remind us that we are not Lone Ranger Christians, left to our own limited wisdom, free to say whatever we want about God's word. Instead, the church that has existed before us and that will still be here after we die has articulated important creedal affirmations that shape, guide, and protect our readings by hemming them within orthodoxy. So a robust reading of Scripture will not pit *informational* skills and readings against *theological* ones, or vice versa. Both are needed for good biblical interpretation.

The Third Stage of the Journey

Transformational Reading with Taylor

YOU ARE HERE

The Third Stage: Transformational Reading with Taylor

- The Goal of Reading Scripture
- Side Trip 5: Metaphors We Read By
- The Posture of Reading Scripture
- Side Trip 6: Knowing through Rituals
- The Holy Spirit in Reading Scripture

We've now reached the third stage of our journey, and Taylor is getting behind the wheel. She has listened attentively to her friends Ingrid and Tom as they have discussed how to read the Bible with informational skills and theological understanding. She agrees. But the whole time she is waiting to ask, "OK, so what?" What do we do with the things we learn from Scripture? Taylor is going to direct us to think about the transforming power and purpose of God's Word.

ORIENTATION

The *transformational* aspect of reading the Bible focuses on the overall purpose of our journey. Without a clear understanding of the direction we are going, we'll never get there. But Scripture is clear what our goal is—being transformed more into God's image. This can be described as growing in love for God and for others, according to Jesus's explanation of God's will for humanity.

Understanding the transformational aspect of our journey involves exploring our goal in reading Scripture, the importance of our posture toward God, and the crucial role that the Holy Spirit plays in interpretation.

Filling Up the Tank

Taylor loves to read Saint Augustine (AD 354–430), the single-most influential theologian of the church's history. And so when Taylor gets behind the wheel for the third stage of our journey, she drops one of her favorite quotes: "So if it seems to you that you have understood the divine scriptures, or any part of them, in such a way that by this understanding you do not build up this twin love of God and neighbor, then you have not yet understood them."[1]

What Augustine is saying here is bold. Let's make sure we understand his claim. Jesus taught that the first and second greatest commandments are related. The first is to love God wholly and the second is to love others (Matt. 22:34–40). Building on this foundation, Augustine argued that since this twin love is God's will for us, this must be the end result of our reading of Scripture. The logic is flawless. Augustine pulls it all together by stating the obvious consequence: we haven't really understood the Bible if this understanding doesn't work itself out in love in our lives.

This is the heart of what Taylor will help us see as we traverse the final stage of our journey toward knowing God through Scripture. Our interpretation of the Bible is not confined to informational skills and theological understanding; it must include and conclude with real life transformation. Interpreting the Bible and applying the Bible are not really separate acts. Any reading or interpretation that doesn't result in life transformation shows itself to be an incomplete and inferior reading, no matter how skilled it is. Our reading must include being transformed in how we think, what we love, and how we live in our bodies. This is not an afterthought or tack on to the informational and theological stages of our journey. If you travel two-thirds of the way toward your destination on a road trip and stop, you haven't arrived, no matter how enjoyable the trip has been.

While she's driving us to our destination, Taylor will help us understand our goal of reading Scripture, the importance of our posture when doing so, and the role of the Holy Spirit in our interpretation. Along the way we'll also take a couple of fascinating side trips to explore the metaphorical nature of language and how our habits affect our knowing.

YOU ARE HERE

The Third Stage: Transformational Reading with Taylor
- **The Goal of Reading Scripture**
- Side Trip 5: Metaphors We Read By
- The Posture of Reading Scripture
- Side Trip 6: Knowing through Rituals
- The Holy Spirit in Reading Scripture

The Goal of Reading Scripture

What is our goal in reading Scripture? We rarely ask ourselves this question, but it's an important one. What we shoot for determines where we will end up. If we aim too low or in the wrong direction, we won't hit the target. Having a clear goal in our minds and hearts affects the vector and altitude of our interpretation of the Bible.

We've already seen one helpful way to answer this question from Augustine: we read the Bible with the goal of expanding the twin loves in our lives. Good interpretation results in greater love for God and for our fellow humans. This is good. This answer focuses on the outcomes, and these are the greatest two outcomes of Bible reading because they are the first and second greatest commandments from God himself. But we can drill down more deeply and speak more specifically about what this great double love looks like. All of this goes under the general heading of *application*.

Receiving the Bible as more than a mere human book—as God speaking truth into our lives—is an essential part of what it means to be a Christian. But unfortunately, in modern times this personal applicational reading has been divorced from our interpretive practices. We separate this fundamental truth into an additional step called application, as if it were an add-on to interpretation. Far better is to recognize that applying the Bible to our own lives is baked into all that we are doing in interpretation. Application is the shaping goal that guides our interpretive habits.

One of the most important biblical texts about the nature of the Bible is 2 Timothy 3:16–17: "All Scripture is breathed out by God and profitable for teaching, for reproof, for correction, and for training in righteousness, that the man of God may be complete, equipped for every good work." These verses give us an incredibly high view of the Bible, identifying it as God's own speech. But we can't stop with this claim.

Identifying Scripture as God's very words is not the main point of these verses but is the basis for Paul's main point—that Scripture's purpose is to teach, reprove, and correct us. All of this can be summed up in that beautiful phrase, "training in righteousness." That is, God is shaping us to inhabit the world in ways that accord with his own ways (righteousness), all for our good. And the end goal of this retraining is that we might become mature or complete ("equipped for every good work"), doing good in the world. The goal of reading Scripture is a transformed life so that we might be God's agents of transformation in the world. As Jesus says, "Let your light shine before others, so that they may see your good works and give glory to your Father who is in heaven" (Matt. 5:16).

Brian Daley, a leading scholar of early church interpretation, notes this important difference between the reading practices of earlier Christianity and our tendency in the modern period. Spiritual reading of Holy Scripture "receives it not simply as a historical document but as a revelation of God's will to heal and transform the hearer." The concern of the ancient interpreters was not primarily to understand the historical situation of the text but how Scripture speaks into the situation of our lives. The "hearers' faith is the living context in which its scriptural meaning—its meaning for our salvation—is to be found."[2]

Also taking a cue from premodern interpretation, the scholar Margaret Mitchell observes that for earliest Christianity, the focus of Scripture study was on the end goal of what would be *beneficial* for the reader. The real spiritual *benefit* of a particular interpretation was recognized as the crucial factor in determining the best of the many possible ways of reading a passage of Scripture. On this basis Mitchell articulates the task of our own reading of the Bible to be "maintaining a carefully calibrated balance among three cardinal virtues of ancient textual interpretation": a close examination of what the text says in whole and part, an awareness of the benefit for present readers, and clemency or charity that seeks to keep the two in balance.[3]

The first of these parts is described with the Greek word *akribeia* which can be defined as "the whole-hearted attention to what the text says, a rigorous application of the human mind and self to the task of . . . preparing the text *for human consumption and delectation*."[4] This is certainly where we start—Ingrid (informational reading) and Tom (theological reading) should be on the trip. We learn to pay close attention to what the texts of Scripture are saying. But this habit and these friends provide the means to a greater end, to a spiritually beneficial and transformational reading. The most important question to ask is this: how does this text benefit my soul and the lives of others? Taylor's transformational focus is nonnegotiable.

An Encounter with God

And now we have come full circle to the insights from Eugene Peterson we began with when we talked about informational reading. Our goal in reading Scripture must be so much *more* than an accurate, intellectual interpretation. We cook with these skills so that we can have an intimate meal with God himself, feasting our souls on all God is for us in Christ Jesus.

One theologian who has written about the importance of application is Timothy Ward.[5] In his thoughtful book on the nature of Scripture and how Scripture relates to God, Ward concludes with a chapter called "The Bible and Christian Life: The Doctrine of Scripture Applied."[6] Ward rightly states that "the most appropriate question to ask ourselves when we read Scripture is: *What is God wanting to do to me, and in me, through the words I am reading?*"[7] He notes that this does not imply that the text means simply whatever it means to me, because Scripture is God speaking and saying something to us.

However, reading the Bible is not just about understanding what the text says. "Interpretation should serve only to lead us to an encounter with God as he actually presents himself to us in Scripture."[8] That's well said—reading the Bible is an encounter with God. If our reading of Scripture stops at the comprehension stage, then as Ward points out, we have made the mistake of exalting Scripture's content over its purpose, ripping apart what God has put together. Therefore the fundamental question we ask when reading the Bible is what is the Lord wanting to *do* with that teaching in us?

Similarly, J. I. Packer, the author of a wonderful book on knowing God, gives this important challenge as we think about our goal in reading Scripture:

> To approach Bible study with no higher a motive than a desire to know all the answers is the direct route to a state of self-satisfied self-deception. . . . there can be no spiritual health without

doctrinal knowledge; but it is equally true that there can be no spiritual health *with* it, if it is sought for the wrong purpose and valued by the wrong standard.[9]

We need to read the Bible wisely and with doctrinal knowledge, but this alone is insufficient. Indeed, it may harm us, leading us into the dangerous waters of self-deception. The wise course is to read with diligence—informationally with Ingrid and theologically with Tom—but always with the end goal of transformation in mind.

Four Questions

Daniel Doriani has been a professor and a pastor for many decades. He has written a very helpful book on the topic of biblical interpretation.[10] But he noticed that even though evangelicals write a lot of books on interpretation, we write very few on application, as if we assume that applying the Bible is intuitive or natural. But it is not. All of the different parts and genres of Scripture are useful to teach and train us (2 Tim. 3:16–17), but they aren't necessarily applied in the same way. In his book dedicated to the application of the Bible, Doriani identifies four questions that we can use to shape and deepen application of all parts of the Bible.[11] These four questions—and the form of application that each addresses—are

- What should I do? Duty
- Who am I? Character
- Where should we go? Goals
- How can I see? Discernment

Duty is the easiest and the most dangerous form of application. It is the easiest because you can base it on straightforward commands from God in the Bible: don't lie, don't commit adultery or idolatry, and so on. God does command us to do certain things and not to do other things, always for our good. However, we still need wisdom to know *how* to specifically apply God's commands to real-life situations. All would agree that "you shall not murder" (Exod. 20:13) applies to premeditated serial killing. But how does it apply in situations of self-defense or war? The interpreter's work of application is not done by simply reading or restating what the Bible commands. And this leads to why duty application is the most dangerous form of application. It can easily result in authoritarian legalism with no nuance or sensitivity to real-life complexities. Yes, the Bible often speaks to what we should do, but this requires wisdom to know how certain commands work out in various situations. Duty is not a sufficient approach to applying Scripture to our lives. We also need other types of application.

Character application focuses on what kind of people God is shaping us to be. God cares not for mere duty-based and external-only obedience (Ps. 51:16–17; Isa. 29:13; Hos. 6:6). He wants us to be whole people who are growing to be more like him (Lev. 19:2; Matt. 5:48).[12] To be godly is to be growing in godlikeness; "godly" is just a shortened form for "godlike."[13] We will always be distinct from God because he is the Creator and we are merely limited, fallen creatures. But we are made in his image, and we are being remade into his image through Jesus Christ (Rom. 12:1–2; 2 Cor. 3:18). All of this can be called virtue or character. Because the transformation of our character (our whole person) is God's goal in our redemption, character is central to the application of the Bible to ourselves. So whenever we read the Bible we should ask, what kind of person does God want me to become through the application of this text to my life? As Doriani observes, duty tells us to do the right thing. Character tells us that righteous people do the right things, focusing on developing who they are so that they might know the right thing to do. We need to focus on character in application because commands and laws "cannot fully map the Christian life."[14] Through character-based wisdom we become the kind of people who know what to do in any given circumstance.

Goals are the application of Scripture to what motivates us; they are why we do one thing and not another. Regardless of whether we realize it, we all have goals, large and small, that drive our lives. One of the important ways we can apply the Bible is by letting it shape our sensibilities, our desires, our values, and thereby our habits. The way we spend our moments, hours, days, and months is who we are and who we are becoming. The Bible has a lot to say about these motivating goals in our lives. For example, Jesus says, "Where your treasure is, there your heart will be also" (Matt. 6:21), so we should "seek first the kingdom of God and his righteousness" (Matt. 6:33). If instead we lay up treasures on earth rather than with our Father in heaven, the result will be loss and destruction not fullness of life. When we read Scripture we are asking God to shape our life-driving goals.

Discernment application is similar to goal application in that we are asking God to apply Scripture to our lives by showing us how to "discriminate between biblical and unbiblical voices within the competing worldviews we encounter."[15] Discernment is the applied wisdom that helps us interpret the world and ourselves clearly in light of God's overall teaching in Scripture. A key way that the Bible applies to us is by revealing our tendency to adopt habits, beliefs, and desires that are not rooted in God and his word.

Thus, the application of the Bible to our lives—the goal of reading Scripture—is varied and requires that we learn to ask questions about different aspects of who we are. Doriani helpfully sums it up this way: "Duty stresses what we ought to do, character examines who we ought to be, goals touch what we ought to seek, and discernment explores competing ideas about God, duty and character."[16]

YOU ARE HERE

The Third Stage: Transformational Reading with Taylor
- The Goal of Reading Scripture
- **Side Trip 5: Metaphors We Read By**
- The Posture of Reading Scripture
- Side Trip 6: Knowing through Rituals
- The Holy Spirit in Reading Scripture

Side Trip 5: Metaphors We Read By

Mary Hirsch cleverly quipped, "Humor is a rubber sword—it allows you to make a point without drawing blood."[17]

This is a metaphor, a figure of speech in which one idea is combined with another idea to create a new and stimulating understanding. Hirsch's metaphor is meaningful because it's not tired and clichéd and because it bears fruit (another metaphor) in our minds. It evokes a mental visual image and also immediately rings true (another metaphor; sorry, I'll stop). We can think of several ways that using humor in an argument is helpfully analogous to using a rubber sword: it makes the disagreement less violent, leaves no scar, doesn't evoke a greater response, doesn't kill. Nevertheless, humor does *do* something; it makes a point—complete with a nice double meaning of "point" as an idea within an argument and the tip of the (rubber) sword. This is a great metaphor, demonstrating the use of human language at the height of its God-given power.

Note also two further aspects of the effectiveness of this (and any good) metaphor. First, it is embedded in our cultural and personal experience. The reason this metaphor works (at least for me) is that I know what a sword is, what it does, and how rubber behaves. This is not just a function of my knowing the vocabulary words "sword" and "rubber" but my having embodied personal and cultural experiences that activate the metaphor. For this metaphor to work I need some prior experience (physically and/or mentally) with swords, attacks, and with objects made of rubber. These things are all combined in unexpected ways, enabling me to imagine something I had not before. But it immediately works because I have a frame of understanding based on experiences.

Second, notice that the metaphor can't be reduced to its propositional idea, at least not without losing its power, nor can it be paraphrased or translated into another image without changing what it says. If we try to boil the sentence down to what it *really* says, we end up with—not a truer or more effective utterance—but a weaker and less powerful one. In fact, it is difficult to determine what exactly a paraphrased version should be: "Humor can make an argument that does not kill someone." That doesn't quite get it. "Humor in an argument helps you articulate something without hurting the other's feelings, escalating the conflict, or wounding another's psyche." That conveys the idea partially but not wholly and certainly not without the same verve and power.

This is the nature of metaphors. By combining two or more images / experiences / ideas, a host of helpful and insightful connections are made in the hearer's mind. You really can't reduce or paraphrase the metaphor without killing it (another metaphor; this time I'll really stop). And a different image combination would produce a different meaning and set of evocations that can't be equated. If we said, "Humor is a paper tank," or, "Humor is an unloaded gun," or, "Humor is a broken trebuchet," although these war metaphors communicate similar ideas, they can only do so partially and with a different set of emotional resonances and mental images.

This is but one example of a metaphor, a basic component of language that fills our speech, our lives, and our Bibles. Much more could be said about how metaphors work.[18]

Let me point out a couple of the ways that understanding metaphor-power is helpful for a good reading of the Bible. First, we need to pay closer attention to how the Bible communicates in metaphors and not try to reduce those to merely propositional statements. Each metaphor—for example, God as Father or as shelter—has a power that cannot be translated into another image or statement without losing some of its purpose. Every metaphor both hides and highlights some aspects of the reality being imperfectly described. To say God is Father is to highlight some aspects of his character and how he relates to humanity, but this metaphor cannot fully describe who he is. We cannot reduce this to saying simply that he is father-like. When we start paying attention to the many metaphors in the Bible, we can resist the temptation toward reductionism and embrace the multifaceted ways the Bible is communicating.

Second, we are reminded that God is a speaking God who uses our embodied experiences and cultural situatedness to communicate to us. Thus, our reading will never be perfect and can always be improved as we grow in experience and self-awareness. This reminds us of the importance of the many skills we learned from Ingrid about historical and cultural context. Metaphors are powerful language tools that make abstract ideas concrete. But they can only do so through shared, culturally based and embodied experiences. Many of these experiences transcend ancient culture and make sense to us still today because they are *human* experiences, not merely cultural ones. Nonetheless, we need to pay attention to how metaphors work to benefit from their usage. Returning to the God as Father example, having a father is an experience that most humans can relate to, but this doesn't necessarily mean that our personal experiences with fathers is what the biblical metaphor intends to communicate. In the ancient world the father metaphor primarily communicated the notions of superior protection and provision more than it communicated intimacy.

YOU ARE HERE

The Third Stage: Transformational Reading with Taylor
- The Goal of Reading Scripture
- Side Trip 5: Metaphors We Read By
- **The Posture of Reading Scripture**
- Side Trip 6: Knowing through Rituals
- The Holy Spirit in Reading Scripture

The Posture of Reading Scripture

In the last fifty years, a lot of literary analysts have talked about the role of the reader in interpretation. For many scholars the point has been that texts don't have any meaning *in themselves* but only what readers bring to the words on the page. This is not a Christian understanding of Scripture, which is rooted in the foundational idea that the Bible faithfully communicates God's own voice, his own words. The Bible is not merely a record of human thoughts. It is not a wax nose that we can shape however we want. Scripture is God speaking; it disrupts, invites, and changes us.

But we must also understand that we readers do play a crucial part in the interpretation of the Bible. We don't change the meaning of the biblical text, but our approach and attitude toward the text matters in the act of interpretation. One of the most important things we bring to the Bible can be summed up in one word: *posture*. Our posture—our heart attitude and response—toward God as we read is the key element that goes beyond any set of skills and sensibilities we use in interpretation (whether informational or theological).

Standing under the Word

In the Modern period, scholars have emphasized that method is the key to good biblical interpretation. Once we get the right method and skills, we can make a text reveal its secrets, its meaning. As Joel Green notes, "Modernity has nurtured practices of biblical interpretation oriented toward pinning down the meaning of a biblical text, deciphering it once-and-for-all, mastering and controlling it."[19]

But instead of standing over a text and dissecting it, our posture ought to be one of *standing under* God's Word and submitting to it. The key to understanding is standing under. More than techniques, we need to develop "dispositions and postures and gestures such as acceptance, devotion, attention, and trust."[20] This heart posture and habit of responding is the nonnegotiable part we play in the good interpretation of Scripture.

Our journey of interpretation is not a safari where we travel to the exotic world of the Bible, capture some verses, and bring them back (stuffed and safe) to our comfortable living rooms. Or to use another equally aggressive image, we must not engage in Viking exegesis—sailing our boats up to the shore of the Bible, running in and knocking a few verses over the head, dragging them back to the ship of our lives, and sailing away. Rather, we need to adopt the posture of a pilgrim: we are on a journey toward understanding, looking for guidance and help along the way. The posture of a pilgrim is dependence, humility, and hunger, as we progress toward a goal, seeking to be changed along the way.[21] We arrive on the shores of God's world revealed through God's word, and we unload our belongings, settle in, and begin to explore our new habitation.

Eugene Peterson reminds us that we do not read the Bible and the writings of church history that were shaped by it "in order to find out how to get God into our lives, get him to participate in our lives. No. We open this book and find that page after page it takes us off guard, surprises us, and draws us into *its* reality, pulls us into participation with God on *his* terms."[22]

If Scripture is God speaking to us, then when we are reading the Bible we are not seeking to master the text but to be mastered by it, not merely to understand the text but to stand under it. We are seeking to find our lives through entering into the life of God revealed in Scripture.

The Christian philosopher Søren Kierkegaard wrestled with God and how to apply Scripture in a personal way. He found that the modern approach to the Bible among scholars and even in the church was deeply problematic if one wanted to actually encounter God through Scripture. Scholarly, highly skilled methods applied to the Bible can often be used to distract the reader from God himself. Scripture is like a love letter from God to us directly and should be received as such. Kierkegaard was not opposed to tools when they help us understand the Bible's message. But the disposition of the interpreter was the essential (and often missing) element. "Kierkegaard would rather see Denmark give all its Bibles back to God than perpetuate a situation in which the Bible is approached as a historical curiosity, an aesthetic masterpiece, or even a doctrinal compendium, rather than for what it really is: the 'highway signs' pointing to Christ, the way of truth and life."[23]

Lectio Divina

The posture of Christians in the first several centuries of the church provides a good model for us. For the earliest Christians, salvation was not understood as simply an act of the past but the ongoing process of ever changing to become more like God himself, for his image to be restored in us (Rom. 8:29). Because of this proper emphasis, growing in God-centered virtue is the aim of interpretation. Openness to be changed is the necessary posture in reading. As Hans Boersma notes, the church fathers understood the Christian life as a journey into ever-deeper communion with God, with Scripture as the guide. Therefore, "any interpretation that does not lead to growth in virtuous habits is, according to patristic exegesis, not interpretation worthy of God."[24]

One of my theology professors used to open class with this great prayer that reveals and shapes a proper posture when we read the Bible: "Lord, open your word to us, and open us to your word." We need the Holy Spirit to enable us to understand Scripture (more on this below), but we also need our hearts opened to imbibing and applying what we come to understand. Thomas à Kempis sums up well the importance of this humble stance: "What good does it do to speak learnedly about the Trinity if, lacking humility, you displease the Trinity?"[25]

To make this reading posture more than a theory, ancient Christians often practiced what is called *lectio divina* ("divine reading").[26] *Lectio divina* is a practiced mode of Scripture reading that is intentionally ever conscious of God's presence. It is not magical or mystical but simply prayerful and reflective, a perfect posture for reading Holy Scripture. *Lectio divina* involves four steps that can be thought of as four orienting compass points: reading (*lectio*), meditating on what has been read (*meditatio*), praying to God (*oratio*), and contemplation, a time of reflective silence that is attentive to God (*contemplatio*).

Lectio is a slow, thoughtful, careful reading of a text, looking for words or phrases that catch your eye. *Meditatio* reads the text again and returns to those phrases or particular verses to ponder them, letting them roll around on your tongue and in your heart. It is easy at this point to fall back into an analytical study mode, but you should resist this. This is prayerful meditation, opening yourself to what God might be saying through certain verses or phrases. Next we turn our thoughts and words directly to God in *oratio*, prayer. This may be silent prayer, or better, if you are alone, speaking to God aloud about what he is saying through Scripture. You may also want to write down your prayers as a way of journaling and remembering them. Finally, and this can be the most difficult step for our phone-filled, fast-paced lives, you sit in silent reflection, *contemplatio*. Reflection is not praying directly to God or filling your mind with new thoughts, but disciplining yourself to sit silently, paying attention to how these revealed truths may impact your soul. Your mind will wander, but like any discipline, you can get better at learning to sit still and be quiet.

At a retreat recently I was part of a group that engaged (individually but all in the same room) in *lectio divina* on Psalm 16. This short psalm is very personal and directed as a prayer of hope, praise, and trust in God. In repeatedly reading and meditating on the psalm, I was struck by several beautiful phrases, but especially, "You are my Lord; / I have no good apart from you" (Ps. 16:2). I have continued to meditate on this life-shaping truth for a couple of months now. By slowing down, paying attention, and meditating on one phrase (not just checking off Ps. 16 on a Bible reading plan), my heart and faith have been enlarged, and I have been redirected to "seek first the kingdom of God and his righteousness" (Matt. 6:33) in many moments of discouragement and temptation.

TAKE A TURN AT THE WHEEL

Read Psalm 51. Now read it again, more slowly. This is a prayer of confession. Go back through it again, not just reading each line but saying them out loud in prayer to God. Pause after each line and slowly meditate on what you've read.

YOU ARE HERE

The Third Stage: Transformational Reading with Taylor

- The Goal of Reading Scripture
- Side Trip 5: Metaphors We Read By
- The Posture of Reading Scripture
- **Side Trip 6: Knowing through Rituals**
- The Holy Spirit in Reading Scripture

Side Trip 6: Knowing through Rituals

For many modern Christians "ritual" is a bad word, communicating something that is old-fashioned, tiresome, obligatory, and therefore meaningless. Certainly there are rituals that fit this description, especially if they are completely disconnected from real life.

However, this negative view of rituals obscures a deeper truth. In reality we are fundamentally *ritualized* creatures: almost everything we do is a ritual, a habit, a way of doing things that we learned somewhere. How you brush your teeth, where you put your phone at night, where you shop, what you do during a long car ride—everything has rituals underneath it, guiding our actions.

And here's the most shocking thing: rituals don't just reveal what we value and who we are; rituals shape who we become. The relationship between our rituals and us is a two-way street. Rituals both reflect and affect who we are. Rituals reflect what we know and care about, and they shape what we know and care about. As the anthropologist Catherine Bell notes, "Kneeling does not merely *communicate* subordination [to outside observers]. . . . Kneeling produces a subordinated kneeler in and through the act itself."[27] As we do, so we become. We are ritualized creatures as God made us.

What does our ritualized nature have to do with reading the Bible well? Recognizing that we are made as ritual creatures helps us understand that when God commands us to engage in regular practices, he knows that these will shape us for our good. Baptism, partaking in the Lord's Table, confessing our sins to him and to each other, singing, praying, lamenting, serving others, giving money and time to help those in need, reading the Bible—any of these practices could be (and often are) written off as mere "rituals" or practiced legalistically. But this is our mistake if we do. These habits are meant to shape us. When we trust God enough to let him guide our habits, then we will see that his wisdom blesses us. It's really another example of the invitation to "come and see," to "taste and see that the Lord is good." Only in the *doing* of what God tells us will we really come to *understand* what he is saying and that it is good.

Foundational to all of this ritualized understanding is reading, studying, and meditating on Scripture. God's word is where we learn what he commands us. So as we read and then practice his commands, we will be shaped into different people, to grow in wisdom, peace, and flourishing. This is what we saw in Psalm 1 earlier. The flourishing person is the one who engages in the habit, the ritual, of meditating on God's word. The result of this practice is personal transformation (or destruction for those who do not).

Studying Scripture is a habit, one you can get better at. Maybe reading is difficult for you. Maybe paying attention is hard. If so, this is almost certainly a function of the ways our technology has ritualized our attention span to crave quick and easy dopamine hits. But the good news about being ritualized creatures is that we can change. Through intentionally developing other habits we can redirect our lives and our experience. Our habits shape us to see and to be in the world differently. So lean into how God has made you as a creature of habit and trust him enough to step toward his good commands.

To get very practical, at night try plugging in your phone on the other side of the room instead of next to your bed. Rather than looking at your phone before you go to sleep, have a Bible next to your bed. Even if you only read a few verses, this little change can have a huge impact. Do likewise when you wake up in the morning. Maybe if you've been practicing *lectio divina*, you have written down some verses on notecards. Why not meditate on those before you go to sleep and when you wake up? These kinds of small, ritualized habits will shape you to become a different kind of person.

YOU ARE HERE

The Third Stage: Transformational Reading with Taylor
- The Goal of Reading Scripture
- Side Trip 5: Metaphors We Read By
- The Posture of Reading Scripture
- Side Trip 6: Knowing through Rituals
- **The Holy Spirit in Reading Scripture**

The Holy Spirit in Reading Scripture

On our journey toward understanding Scripture we have seen that skills, theology, and our posture are all essential ingredients. But we must consider one more fundamental reality as we seek to encounter God through the Bible: the necessary role of God's own Spirit.

Illumination

Christians have always understood that the Bible is Spirit-wrought and God-breathed (2 Tim. 3:16; 2 Pet. 1:21). Scripture is inspired or spirated, coming from the Holy Spirit's work in and through human authors. But the Holy Spirit's role does not stop with the writing of the texts. Good interpretation is also dependent on the ongoing work of the Spirit to in-*spire* us to understand, receive, and apply what God has spoken. We call this the doctrine of *illumination* of the Holy Spirit.

I mentioned above my old theology professor's prayer: "Lord, open your word to us, and open us to your word." The first part of this excellent prayer addresses the fundamental need for the Spirit's work in our understanding of the Bible. We need the word to be opened to us. The good news is that God is willing and glad to grant us Spirit-given understanding, as Jesus himself tells us. We are invited to ask, seek, and knock because our heavenly Father will "give the Holy Spirit to those who ask him" (Luke 11:9–13). This certainly applies to the Spirit's work of illumination.

One of the passages that speaks most clearly and strongly about the role of the Holy Spirit in our understanding is 1 Corinthians 2:1–16. Paul makes clear that everything—from the basic message of the gospel to the deepest theological truths—is bound up with the active work of the Holy Spirit because the Spirit of God alone comprehends the thoughts of God (1 Cor. 2:11). The difference between those who truly understand the Bible's teachings and those who do not isn't based on education, skill set, or intelligence. It's a *spiritual* matter. The Spirit reveals, instructs, and enables us to apply the beautiful and mysterious teachings of Scripture to our own lives.

I remember when I was in seminary that I wrestled with how to fit this truth together with the writings of many biblical scholars who were not Christians. I have benefitted from and continue to learn much from many scholars who are not Spirit-filled believers. They often have great insights into various aspects of the Bible, including historical background, grammar, literary structure, inner-biblical connections, and even application. The Spirit's role in illumination does not eliminate or minimize these insights. We could put these under the category of common grace given to all of God's creatures. Additionally, there is a difference between knowledge about the Bible and the Spirit-given wisdom that perceives and embraces the reality of which the Bible speaks (1 Cor. 2:6, 13). A nonspiritual person, what Paul calls "the natural person" (1 Cor. 2:14), may perceive certain things about God and the Bible (as Rom. 1 points out), but that person will not be able to receive and accept these things as the truth apart from the illuminating work of the Holy Spirit.

The inability of unbelievers to embrace Scripture is related to the doctrine of the witness of the Holy Spirit through Scripture. Protestant theologians have especially emphasized that the Holy Spirit's work in us ultimately convinces us of the truthfulness of Scripture. As the Westminster Confession states, "Our full persuasion and assurance of the infallible truth and divine authority thereof, is from the inward work of the Holy Spirit bearing witness by and with the Word in our hearts."[28] Theologian J.V. Fesko comments on this helpfully:

> In other words, fallen sinners will never humbly submit to the word of God. Rather, the Holy Spirit must first convict sinners of their need for repentance so that they will trust in Christ for their salvation. Once the Spirit has tamed our sinful hearts, we no longer come to the Scriptures with malice and rebellion but as hungry children seeking bread from our heavenly Father.[29]

Knowing is a spiritual matter—experiencing God through the work of the Holy Spirit. The Puritan theologian John Owen said it well:

> That Jesus Christ was crucified, is a proposition that any natural man may understand and assent to, and be said to receive: and all the doctrines of the gospel may be taught in propositions

and discourses, the sense and meaning of which a natural man may understand; but it is denied that he can receive the things themselves. For there is a wide difference between the mind's receiving doctrines notionally, and receiving the things taught in them really.[30]

We began this book with John 1 where Jesus invited people to "come and see." This was an embedded lesson in biblical interpretation. Following Jesus by faith (i.e., discipleship) is the foundation of understanding. We don't simply understand and then follow. We come to understand as we follow. This is the work of the Spirit.

At the end of Jesus's earthly ministry, on his last night with his disciples, he revisits the matter of how to understand what God is saying to the world. And the key once again is the Holy Spirit. Jesus tells his disciples—who continue in succession down to us today—that after his departure the Father and he will send the Spirit of truth who will reside in and among believers (John 14:16–17). This person of God, the Holy Spirit, will "teach you all things and bring to your remembrance all that I have said to you" (14:26). The Spirit will testify to the world who Jesus is (15:26), which certainly includes empowering the written testimony in Scripture. The Spirit will bring conviction on the world (16:8–10). Jesus taught his disciples much, but there was more to be said and more to teach the world (now recorded in the New Testament). The Spirit of truth will do this work. The Spirit will speak what Jesus says and glorify him (16:12–15).

This spiritual reality means that we must begin and end and saturate all our interpretation of Scripture with a conscious dependence on the Holy Spirit to enable us to understand and apply it. For me this typically means getting on my knees before opening the Bible and asking God to reveal himself to me. This physical posture is not necessary, but it helpfully communicates to my mind and body that my reading of Scripture is a deeply spiritual activity.

Here's a great prayer from Thomas Aquinas that reflects this understanding and can helpfully guide our study of Scripture:

> Ineffable Creator, Who out of the treasures of Thy wisdom hast appointed three hierarchies of Angels and set them in admirable order high above the heavens and hast disposed the divers portions of the universe in such marvelous array, Thou Who art called the True Source of Light and super-eminent Principle of Wisdom, be pleased to cast a beam of Thy radiance upon the darkness of my mind and dispel from me the double darkness of sin and ignorance in which I have been born.
>
> Thou Who makest eloquent the tongues of little children, fashion my words and pour upon my lips the grace of Thy benediction. Grant me penetration to understand, capacity to retain, method and facility in study, subtlety in interpretation and abundant grace of expression. Order the beginning, direct the progress and perfect the achievement of my work, Thou who art true God and Man and livest and reignest for ever and ever. Amen.[31]

Bounded Pluriformity

Scripture in its richness and depth contains a *bounded pluriformity of meaning*. This means that while Scripture does have a definitive message from God, this message is layered and manifold. In any text of Scripture there are many good, powerful, and true things being said. Additionally, there are many things that can be said by synthesizing many parts of Scripture together (what we call doing theology). Informational, theological, and transformational readings result in a variety of true statements. The Holy Spirit's role is to guide us—both individually and corporately—to hear, receive, and apply aspects of this rich truth in our own contexts. This is in fact what theology really is—reading the whole of Scripture for understanding and application *for today.*

There is a beautiful tension and balance to be maintained in all of this. Every generation, culture, and place must write their own Spirit-led, contextualized theology while these theological statements are simultaneously bounded by the greater tradition of Christian truth (found most easily in the creeds). How a text of Scripture is read and applied in Nairobi, New York, and Nanjing will inevitably vary, and this is OK.

The same is true for reading and interpreting Scripture. The Spirit guides us to read, understand, and apply Scripture within our own context (how could we understand it in any other way?), while at the same time our reading is bound and circumscribed by the tradition of Christian orthodoxy. Within this bounded pluriformity of Scripture the Spirit is at work in and through us.

This brings us back to our earlier discussion about the helpmate role of the church's tradition while reading Scripture. As we noted above, Scripture is ultimately authoritative on its own, but we also need help from others in reading Scripture well; there is no virtue in being a Lone Ranger interpreter. The Holy Spirit has guided his people within the church to understand the truth and to communicate its teachings well. The creeds and the tradition of orthodoxy are central ways in which the Holy Spirit guides and shapes our reading of Scripture. As the Reformer John Calvin noted, for those who have God as their Father, the church serves as the mother, nurturing and guiding our reading of the Bible.[32]

So while we may be inclined to think that Taylor's role in our company of travelers is secondary or maybe not as weighty as that of Ingrid or Tom, it turns out that without Taylor's driving we would actually never get to where we are going: encountering God. The ultimate sense of transformational reading comes from the Holy Spirit's work in us.

TAKE A TURN AT THE WHEEL

Get on your knees and read Ephesians 3:14–19. Now read it aloud, slowly, prayerfully, pausing after each line to meditate and let the words hang in the air.

What do we learn about God's desires for us? What is Paul praying for believers to experience? Make a list of Paul's requests.

Now pray the prayer again out loud, applying it to yourself and asking God to make these things true of you.

Epilogue

The Final Destination

The long and enjoyable journey is over. Our friends have guided us well, and all three segments of our road trip are complete, including several great side trips. It's time to turn off the engine, unpack our bags, and walk into our destination. (I'll let the reader decide whether this is a mountain cabin or a beach house.) Now that we have arrived, it will be good to reflect backwards on what we have experienced and look forward to what we will be doing next.

Backward Reflection

As we think back on our journey, a bit of reflection reveals that our three segments are not entirely segmented. That is, while Ingrid, Tom, and Taylor gave the primary direction to their respective portions of the journey, the conversation was never limited to one perspective. The organic human mind and heart is more fluid than that. We can never really separate information, theology, and transformation.

We might even describe this relationship with an old term: *perichoretic*. This Greek word means to rotate, or go around, as in a dance. Imagine a social dance where people are following coordinated moves while changing partners. As we read Scripture in this threefold way, we are being led and guided by different partners who teach us to move with the rhythm of Scripture. And at the same time we move seamlessly from one dance and one partner to another.

So too with the informational, theological, and transformational aspects of the good reading of Scripture. While it is often helpful to approach the biblical texts in a stairstep way, wrestling with the informational content, reflecting theologically, and then articulating transformational points, the reality is that these three distinct approaches are constantly informing one another and are ultimately inseparable. It is one dance.

The ancient adage that one cannot tell which came first, the chicken or the egg, appears again here: when we interpret a text of Scripture, we cannot and should not think of this happening in a lockstep manner, depending entirely on the preceding step. Rather, the informational, theological, and transformational aspects are actually occurring in us simultaneously. One mode of reading does not really create the others. They are all mutually informing, or dancing, together.

For example, how we decide on the most relevant information in a text is determined by the kinds of questions we are asking. When we ask questions of character-formation, this shapes what we see as relevant in the content. Likewise, broader theological convictions that come from the whole canon and creedal affirmations shape our understanding of the role of linguistic and historic information in the text. At the same time, gaining new cultural and historical information challenges our traditional ways of interpreting these cherished texts. Our reading in each of these three ways—for information, for theology, for transformation—exist in a circular, mutually informing and mutually symbiotic relationship.

Case Study: Jesus as God—
Arianism versus Orthodox Christianity

"Jesus is *a* son of God, but not the only one, and being a son of God does *not* make a person divine. Every believer is a son of God. Jesus was a godly prophet, but we dishonor God if we say Jesus is God. God is one, not two or three beings."

These words are typical of a certain heretical view of Jesus that goes back to ancient times called Arianism. This view still exists today in some cult groups, such as the Jehovah's Witnesses. They interpret the words of John 1:1 very differently than the orthodox Christian tradition: "In the beginning was the Word, and the Word was with God, and the Word was a god" (New World Translation). They explain their view this way: "The phrase 'the Word was a god' describes the divine or godlike nature that Jesus possessed before he came to earth. He can be described in this way because of his role as God's Spokesman and his unique position as the firstborn Son of God through whom God created all other things."[1]

This may sound like orthodoxy, but the explanation on the official Jehovah's Witnesses website notes that Jesus is substantively different from God in that Jesus had a beginning, unlike God:

> The "beginning" referred to in this verse cannot mean "the beginning" of God because God had no beginning. Jehovah God is "from everlasting to everlasting." (Psalm 90:1, 2) However, the Word, Jesus Christ, did have a beginning. He is "the beginning of the creation by God."—Revelation 3:14.[2]

Our perichoretic, three-way approach helps us translate and interpret this verse very differently (as most translations render it): "In the beginning was the Word, and the Word was with God, and the Word was God."

The *informational* mode of reading enables us to understand how Greek grammar informs the proper translation. The translation "was a god" is based on a basic misunderstanding of how the Greek system of articles ("the"/"a") works. "The Word was God" or "the Word was Divine" are both better translations than the misleading "the Word was a god." But this kind of reading is not enough.

The *theological* reading approach gives us the canonical perspective, the theological framework, and the historical tradition to help us understand Arianism and its problems, in addition to unlocking the profound richness of the orthodox Trinitarian understanding. The witness of the whole biblical canon shows us, for example, how Jesus's actions uniquely line up with those actions that are only the prerogative of God. Jesus is repeatedly shown by his words and actions to share the divine identity of God. His enemies are right to accuse him of blasphemy because of what he said and did—unless he is indeed God! Additionally, from the earliest days of the church Christians have written creeds and treatises that help us think through these questions biblically and theologically. To answer the question of Jesus's divinity, we can and should get help from such Christian thinkers and leaders of the past—not just rely on our own limited knowledge. The creeds and theological works of countless thinkers affirm the divine identity of Jesus.

The *transformational* reading of Scripture adds a crucial Spirit-led aspect to our understanding of this issue. As Jesus himself said in John 7:17, "If anyone's will is to do God's will, he will know whether the teaching is from God or whether I am speaking on my own authority." And as the elder John teaches in his famous letter, those who deny the divinity of Jesus eventually leave the true community of God because they are not truly born of God (1 John 2:19). The reality is that our beliefs and our practices in community are mutually informing and affecting each other. Loving one another, for example, both reflects and affects our doctrinal understanding. In other words, understanding Jesus's identity is not just a function of exegetical skills, but is teaching that comes from the Holy Spirit through the church, lived out in community.

The point of this short example is that good reading of the Bible is dependent on a robust, three-mode approach. Every decision about what the Bible is saying should be informed by a deeply triune understanding that comes from multiple approaches to reading, informed by God's church, and inspired by the Holy Spirit.

A Brief Negative Note: What Happens When We Don't Read in the Three Ways?

If this robust three-fold mode of reading happened naturally and was common today, we would not need the book you're holding in your hands. But in reality we often *don't* read this way. And the result is, like trying to sit on a stool with only one leg or filming a movie with a broken tripod, our reading is often imbalanced and unsteady. Or to return to our journey image, what happens if we leave two of our friends behind at a rest stop? What if only Ingrid, Tom, or Taylor makes the trip?

The natural human tendency is to find one way of reading and focus on that to the exclusion of the others. This singular focus may occur because of training, the habits of others around you, or your own skills and interests. If you really enjoy reading history, the historical background approach to reading the Bible will probably appeal to you. Or maybe you are in a church where intentional Bible study isn't part of the culture, and thus you only read devotionally with little guidance. Most imbalanced readings tend to take one of the three aspects to the exclusion of the others.

Some readers, especially in our day, focus all their attention on an informational approach. The result is often educated and rigorous. Historical, linguistic, cultural, and literary insights provide depth and respectability. People feel like they are really growing in Bible knowledge. But without the other modes, this often results in a dry and even argumentative style of reading. In fact, informational-only readers—of both believing and nonbelieving types—are often adamant that good reading is wrapped up in this approach and that everything else is extra or even unhelpful. For unbelieving Bible scholars, this often contains a strong rhetoric that we cannot and should not read the Bible in theological and personal ways, lest we over-interpret it. Believers of this persuasion often put forward an equally strong argument that good reading must separate the meaning (found only through the informational approach) from the significance and application. If we don't, the argument goes, we lack a solid basis for belief.

These are immature versions of Ingrid in which she is a little too self-confident and hasn't had her zeal tempered by real-life experience. She thinks she can drive the whole way, but she can't. Not only is it impossible to read informationally apart from theological and spiritual realities, but it is also not desirable. This is a misunderstanding of the complexity of Scripture, the role of the Spirit in all understanding, and the goal of why we are reading the Bible. While informational interpretation is necessary, it cannot be the exclusive focus of our reading.

Students of the Bible can also mistakenly focus only on a theological reading, spending their time and energy on the good but ultimately too narrow approach of canonical, redemptive-historical, or systematic theological readings. Theology is necessary for a good reading of Scripture, but it can fall prey to two opposite dangers. A theological reading that is not informed by an informational reading can often fail to hear the otherness of the text that textual study provides. That is, we can too easily make Scripture's message a wax nose that fits into our already constructed and desired theological understanding when no attention is given to informational study. Calvinists, Wesleyans, Dispensationalists, Pentecostals all have the tendency to read the Bible in a selective way that affirms their theological views.

On the other hand, a theological reading that does not end in a transformational reading is also dangerous. When we neglect the spiritual and applicational aspect of reading Scripture, regardless of how sound and robust our theological reading is, we fail to read the Bible with the grain of its divinely intended goal. We become theologians that resemble bobble-head figures whose heads are greatly disproportionate to their bodies. We become skilled at the head-knowledge part—debating others on the finer points of doctrine, often expressing great concern that others don't see things the same way as we do. These intense and immature versions of Tom live much of their lives focusing on what's wrong with other people's readings and theological ideas, continually pointing out the dangerous slippery slope of others' positions. This is spiritually unhealthy. As a result, Jesus's twin-love goal is lost.

Finally, we may also note the problem of reading from within a transformational model only. Similar to the problem of a theological reading that lacks informational grounding, many Christians approach Scripture with the right posture and sensitivity to God's voice but come away with readings that lack substance and wisdom. As Peterson rightly warns,

Without exegesis, spirituality gets sappy, soupy. Spirituality without exegesis becomes self-indulgent. Without disciplined exegesis spirituality develops into an idiolect in which I define all the key verbs and nouns out of my own experience. And prayer ends up limping along in sighs and stutters.[3]

Sooner or later, reading for transformation that has no grounding in the other ways of reading will result in little to no true transformation. Taylor has the right heart, but she needs Ingrid and Tom to guide her sinful heart and her inevitably limited understanding (like all of us). Left to her own, Taylor will wander and possibly never reach the destination that she desires.

Nonetheless, in this scenario we must evaluate the potential problem a bit differently. Unlike the other two problematic kinds of readings discussed here, there is a sense in which this transformational-only approach is the least dangerous precisely because of the Holy Spirit's work in and through individual believers and the church. That is, while we would certainly not recommend a Lone Ranger approach that seeks personal application no matter what the text is really saying, in some ways this kind of reading has the most potential to get things right in an imperfect world. This is because God has given teachers to the church, and most importantly the Holy Spirit is at work to guide, correct, and instruct. The sincere reader, like Taylor, who comes to Scripture with a teachable heart has the most important qualification in place. The skill sets and wisdom that come from the informational and theological readings can be learned over time; a receptive and open heart provides the true starting point for the best reading of Scripture.

We can summarize the point in the following table:

What Happens When We Reduce Any of the Reading Modes?

Reduction of Informational Reading	Reduction of Theological Reading	Reduction of Transformational Reading
Readings are often shallow in depth and understanding.	Readings are thin in understanding because they are not informed by the riches of theology.	Readings can become merely intellectual exercises, diconnected from the heart and real life.
Readings become merely sentimental and groundless.	Readings are sub-Christian and miss the overall point of all of Scripture—to reveal God to us.	Readings are sub-Christian and miss the point that all of Scripture is meant to effect change and growth in us.
Scripture becomes a wax nose, saying whatever the reader wants it to say.	Readings are limited and constrained to modernistic approaches to texts.	Applications of Scripture are disconnected from the voice of the text.

Dwelling in Our New Destination

So here we are at the end of the road trip. As it turns out, the destination is really just the beginning. This journey of learning to read Scripture well has brought us to a place where we can continually explore the beautiful vistas and ornate architecture of God's revelation. Our goal on this journey of skill development is not abstract, objectified knowledge about God but God-granted wisdom for how to live our lives.

Knowledge—even knowledge about God—is not an end in itself. Knowledge acquisition serves the purpose of growing in wisdom. Biblical and theological knowledge that does not result in practical moral formation and transformation is merely knowledge and misses the point of theology. The reading of Scripture is always for the purpose of growing in wisdom, not merely in knowledge.

We can sum up the point this way: rather than seeing our goal of biblical interpretation in terms of *mastery*, we need to recapture the Christian idea of *mystery*. We need to rediscover a different posture toward knowing God and the world that he has made. We humbly acknowledge our limited perspective, recognizing that there is significant, impenetrable mystery in our understanding of God and his ways and that our proper response is to be patient sojourners on the journey toward God-centered wisdom.

The juxtaposition of Romans 11 and 12 provides a beautiful picture of this dual reality. In Romans 11 Paul explores one of the single greatest difficulties in the realm of theology, the Bible's teaching about God's sovereignty in saving some people and not others—specifically God's dealings with his covenant people of Israel. After pressing into these truths as far as he can (Rom. 11:1–24), Paul realizes that he has reached the limits of human knowing on such complex and profound issues. He can only respond to this unfathomable *mystery* (11:25–32) with doxology: "Oh, the depth of the riches and wisdom and knowledge of God! How unsearchable are his judgments and how inscrutable his ways!" (11:33). No one has known the mind of the Lord (11:34). All that we can do is to proclaim, "For from him and through him and to him are all things. To him be glory forever. Amen" (11:36). As embodied, limited knowers, this is our humble situation: awe before the mystery and wonder of God.

Romans 11 is followed by the powerful exhortation of Romans 12.1–2:

I appeal to you therefore, brothers, by the mercies of God, to present your bodies as a living sacrifice, holy and acceptable to God, which is your spiritual worship. Do not be conformed to this world, but be transformed by the renewal of your mind, that by testing you may discern what is the will of God, what is good and acceptable and perfect.

Paul is alluding to the sacrificial system that God established as part of his covenant with Israel. Now in the new covenant this image is translated and transformed into the sacrifice of our lives lived for God. This happens through a transformation in our thinking—our knowing—worked out in practical obedience and virtue. The worshiping sacrifice to which God calls us is not the bringing of heifers and doves to the temple, for Christ has perfected and completed this sin-sacrificing system (Heb. 10:1–18). Rather the sacrifice is the offering of our very selves to God by the transformation of our knowledge about who God is. This comes through the renewing of our minds—our whole way of seeing and knowing. Salvation and a proper relationship to God are described in Romans 12:1–2 as the transforming of our knowledge into practical, Christ-centered wisdom. This transformed knowing is the answer to the fundamental problem of sin first identified in Romans 1—the foolish exchange of the knowledge of and glory of God for the knowledge of and worship of created things. Thus, while the bedrock and apex of our knowledge is a *mystery*—a limit to our knowledge—the daily outworking of our Christian lives can be understood very much as a growing in *knowledge* of God in this deeply practical way.

This book is a map not the destination. It's the barn-roof-painted invitation to "See Ruby Falls"; it's not the awesome sight itself. This book and the skills taught herein are only meant to give guidance for studying that *other* book, Scripture, because through it one can meet and know God.

From the earliest days of the church, believers understood that being a disciple of Christ is a lifelong journey. It is not a mere destination attained once a person becomes a Christian—quite the opposite. The eye-opening moment of new birth, repentance, justification (or whatever other biblical metaphor you want to use) is the starting point, not the end point, of the Christian life. For the rest of the journey, the upward expedition of coming to know God, we need maps. The primary means of guidance for our journey is Holy Scripture, illumined by the Holy Spirit. Through this we learn to navigate the perils, valleys, trials, joys, and mountaintops of life. Ingrid, Tom, and Taylor are driving us to the life of daily discipleship.

The truth is that we can't really know something until we practice it, until we experience it with our bodies not just our minds. A few years ago I taught another of my teenagers how to drive a five-speed manual car. I started by explaining what's going on in a transmission and engine, and then I drove around our neighborhood, pointing out what I was doing. The background and theoretical information were helpful. But she couldn't really know what I was talking about until she sat behind the wheel of our old, yellow Xterra and, with starts and stops, tried driving up and down our streets. The same is true with riding a horse, hitting a golf ball straight down the fairway, or holding a loved one's hand as they exhale their last breath—experience alone gives true knowledge of what these things are and mean. So too with God's revealed truth in Scripture. The ultimate knowing of these truths and of God himself can only come through obeying and following—by taking Jesus's yoke on our necks and finding that his ways are gentle, kind, and life-giving (Matt. 11:25–30). The life of being a disciple of Jesus Christ, with all its successes and failures, is the ultimate way to understand Scripture and, thereby, God our Creator himself.

I conclude this discussion of how to read Scripture with an invitation. God created you to experience fullness of life through knowing him. This knowledge comes from a life-long journey that is guided most fully and clearly through Scripture. So even as Jesus said to his first disciples, he is also saying now to us, "Come and see."

Notes

Chapter 1: The First Stage of the Journey: Informational Reading with Ingrid

1. Eugene Peterson, *Eat This Book: A Conversation in the Art of Spiritual Reading* (Grand Rapids, MI: Eerdmans, 2009), 53.
2. For the story of Peterson's life, see Winn Collier, *A Burning in My Bones: The Authorized Biography of Eugene H. Peterson* (Colorado Springs: Waterbrook, 2021).
3. Peterson, *Eat This Book*, 53.
4. Peterson, *Eat This Book*, 55.
5. For a much fuller and more theological exploration of the depth of Handel's composition, one may consult Roger Bullard, *Messiah: The Gospel according to Handel's Oratorio* (Grand Rapids, MI: Eerdmans, 1993) and Calvin Stapert, *Handel's Messiah: Comfort for God's People* (Rapids, MI: Eerdmans, 2010).
6. This example comes from Brennan Breed, "What Is Reception History?," Bible Odyssey, accessed April 1, 2022, https://www.bibleodyssey.org.
7. David Paul Parris, *Reading the Bible with Giants: How 2000 Years of Biblical Interpretation Can Shed New Light on Old Texts*, 2nd ed. (Eugene, OR: Cascade, 2015).
8. Jonathan Pennington, "'Sell You Possessions and Give to the Poor.' A Theological Reflection on Jesus' Teaching Regarding Personal Wealth and Charity," Institute for Faith, Work and Economics, July 9, 2015, https://tifwe.org/wp-content/uploads/2015/07/Sell-Your-Possessions-Reformatted-Pennington.pdf.
9. Peter Turchi, *Maps of the Imagination: The Writer as Cartographer* (San Antonio: Trinity University Press, 2004), 44. For images of both the original London Underground map and Harry Beck's improved map, see "The Genius of the London Tube Map," YouTube video, March 15, 2018, https://www.youtube.com.

10. J. Todd Billings, *The Word of God for the People of God: An Entryway to the Theological Interpretation of Scripture* (Grand Rapids, MI: Eerdmans, 2010), 33.

11. A classic modern text in this area is Gordon Fee and Douglas Stuart, *How to Read the Bible for All Its Worth*, 4th ed. (Grand Rapids, MI: Zondervan Academic, 2014).

12. Thomas R. Schreiner, *40 Questions about Christians and Biblical Law* (Grand Rapids, MI: Kregel, 2010).

13. The Major Prophets are Isaiah, Jeremiah, Ezekiel, and Daniel, along with Lamentations (which is associated with Jeremiah). The Minor Prophets (also known as the Twelve) are Hosea, Joel, Amos, Obadiah, Jonah, Micah, Nahum, Habakkuk, Zephaniah, Haggai, Zechariah, and Malachi.

14. Trevor Hart and Richard Bauckham make the helpful distinction between "imaginative" and "imaginary." Language that is imaginative—using images—is not necessarily lacking a reference to reality. Something can be described imaginatively without being imaginary. Richard Bauckham and Trevor Hart, *Hope against Hope: Christian Eschatology at the Turn of the Millennium* (Grand Rapids, MI: Eerdmans, 1999).

15. The Epistles are generally divided into two parts, the Pauline Epistles (thirteen letters) and the General Epistles (eight letters). The letter to the Hebrews is sometimes included in the General Epistles and sometimes not. For the sake of convenience, I have included it among the eight letters, along with the other non-Pauline letters of James, 1–2 Peter, 1–3 John, and Jude.

16. Mark Allan Powell, *What Do They Hear? Bridging the Gap Between Pulpit and Pew* (Nashville: Abingdon, 2007), 11–28. Thanks to Trevin Wax for first alerting me to this example in his post, "Where You Live Changes What You See When You Read the Bible," The Gospel Coalition, May 28, 2015, https://www.thegospelcoalition.org.

17. For a standard, helpful book exploring this topic, see D. A. Carson, *Exegetical Fallacies*, 2nd ed. (Grand Rapids, MI: Baker Academic, 1996).

Chapter 2: The Second Stage of the Journey: Theological Reading with Tom

1. J. Todd Billings, *The Word of God for the People of God: An Entryway to the Theological Interpretation of Scripture* (Grand Rapids, MI: Eerdmans, 2010), 59.

2. For some helpful further reading on the canon, see Michael J. Kruger, *The Question of Canon: Challenging the Status Quo in the New Testament Debate* (Downers Grove, IL: IVP Academic, 2013).

3. For example, G. K. Beale, *The Temple and the Church's Mission: A Biblical Theology of the Dwelling Place of God* (Downers Grove, IL: IVP Academic, 2004). For a briefer discussion, see G. K. Beale, "Eden, the Temple, and the Church's Mission in the New Creation," *Journal of the Evangelical Theological Society* 48, no. 1 (March 2005): 5–31, https://www.etsjets.org/files/JETS-PDFs/48/48-1/48-1-pp005-031_JETS.pdf.

4. Iain McGilchrist, *The Master and His Emissary: The Divided Brain and the Making of the Western World* (New Haven, CT: Yale University Press, 2009). For an article-length introduction to McGilchrist, see his Iain McGilchrist, *Ways of Attending: How Our Divided Brain Constructs the World* (Oxfordshire, UK: Routledge, 2019).

5. For a helpful exploration of how traditions and liturgies affect our sensibilities, see James K. A. Smith, *Desiring the Kingdom: Worship, Worldview, and Cultural Formation* (Grand Rapids, MI: Baker Academic, 2009).

6. This quotation is often repeated and attributed to Mahler, but I am unable to identify its source.

7. For more on the history of commentaries, see Mark Gignilliat and Jonathan Pennington, "Theological Commentary," in *A Manifesto for Theological Interpretation*, ed. Craig Bartholomew and Heath Thomas (Grand Rapids, MI: Baker Academic, 2016): 237–56.

8. Kevin J. Vanhoozer, *Hearers and Doers: A Pastor's Guide to Making Disciples through Scripture and Doctrine* (Bellingham, WA: Lexham, 2019), 107.

9. Vanhoozer, *Hearers and Doers*, 10.

10. Vanhoozer, *Hearers and Doers*, 133.

11. This section is based on Marc Cortez, *Theological Anthropology: A Guide for the Perplexed* (London: T&T Clark, 2010), 14–40.

12. Surprisingly, there are only two more Old Testament references to the image of God: Gen. 5:1 and 9:6. We also find the idea used indirectly in Ps. 8:4–6. In the New Testament we find several more: 1 Cor. 11:7; 2 Cor. 3:18; 4:4; Eph. 4:24; Col. 1:15; James 3:9.

13. Thankfully this is changing. See Hans Boersma, *Seeing God: The Beatific Vision in Christian Tradition* (Grand Rapids, MI: Eerdmans, 2018) and Michael Allen, *Grounded in Heaven: Recentering Christian Hope and Life on God* (Grand Rapids, MI: Eerdmans, 2018).

14. David Paul Parris, *Reading the Bible with Giants: How 2000 Years of Biblical Interpretation Can Shed New Light on Old Texts*, 2nd ed. (Eugene, OR: Cascade, 2015).

15. Rebekah Eklund, *The Beatitudes through the Ages* (Grand Rapids, MI: Eerdmans, 2021).

16. Many images of this nativity scene can be found online. Try googling "two t. rexes fighting over a table saw."

17. See Georgina Tomlinson, "The Christmas Nativity," The British Postal Museum and Archive Blog, December 18, 2015, https://postalheritage.wordpress.com.

18. See Donald Fairbairn and Ryan M. Reeves, *The Story of Creeds and Confessions: Tracing the Development of the Christian Faith* (Grand Rapids, MI: Baker Academic, 2019). Fairbairn and Reeves explain that the early creeds were relatively short and focused on the Trinity, while later confessions were longer and expanded on issues that derive from faith in the Trinity.

19. J. V. Fesko, *The Need for Creeds Today: Confessional Faith in a Faithless Age* (Grand Rapids, MI: Baker Academic, 2020), xviii [Kindle].

20. Alister E. McGrath, *The Genesis of Doctrine: A Study in the Foundation of Doctrinal Criticism* (Vancouver: Regent College Publishing, 1997), 11–12, as quoted in Joel Green, *Practicing Theological Interpretation: Engaging Biblical Texts for Faith and Formation* (Grand Rapids, MI: Baker Academic, 2011), 71.

21. Among many good discussions that can be found about the rule of faith, one may consult chap. 3 in Green, *Practicing Theological Interpretation*.

22. Billings, *The Word of God for the People of God*, 22.

23. Billings, *The Word of God for the People of God*, 22.

24. Billings, *The Word of God for the People of God*, 12–13.

25. Kevin Vanhoozer, *Hearers and Doers*, 10.

26. There were some differences among various Jewish groups on how they valued different parts of what today we would call the Old Testament canon. The Sadducees, for example, did not value the prophetic writings as much as the Pentateuch. Nonetheless, even with their shared Scriptures, their beliefs varied.

27. Green, *Practicing Theological Interpretation*, 73–74.

28. Irenaeus, *Against Heresies* 1.8.1.

29. In patristic exegesis a common idea is the economy of Scripture—that is, the proper order or structure of the message of the Bible. To understand the economy of Scripture is to understand its scope and driving focus. There are countless good readings that can be generated from thoughtful exegesis, but those that fall outside the economy of Scripture are by definition not Christian readings. See John O'Keefe and Russell Reno, *Sanctified Vision: An Introduction to Early Christian Interpretation of the Bible* (Baltimore: Johns Hopkins University Press, 2005).

30. "The Apostles' Creed," in *Creeds, Confessions, and Catechisms: A Reader's Edition*, ed. Chad Van Dixhoorn (Wheaton, IL: Crossway, 2022), 13.

Chapter 3: The Third Stage of the Journey:
Transformational Reading with Taylor

1. Augustine, *Teaching Christianity (De Doctrina Christiana)*, trans. Edmund Hill, 2nd ed. (Hyde Park, NY: New City, 1995), 1.40.

2. Brian E. Daley, "Is Patristic Exegesis Still Usable?," in *The Art of Reading Scripture*, ed. Ellen F. Davis and Richard B. Hays (Grand Rapids, MI: Eerdmans, 2003), 77.

3. Margaret Mitchell, *Paul, the Corinthians and the Birth of Christian Hermeneutics* (Cambridge: Cambridge University Press, 2010), 108.

4. Mitchell, *Paul*, 108. Italics mine.

5. The following two paragraphs are based on Jonathan Pennington, *Reading the Gospels Wisely: A Narrative and Theological Introduction* (Grand Rapids, MI: Baker Academic, 2012), 155.

6. Timothy Ward, *Words of Life: Scripture as the Living and Active Word of God* (Downers Grove, IL: IVP Academic, 2009).

7. Ward, *Words of Life*, 174–175.

8. Ward, *Words of Life*, 175.

9. J. I. Packer, *Knowing God* (Downers Grove, IL: InterVarsity Press, 1993), 22.

10. Daniel M. Doriani, *Getting the Message: A Plan for Interpreting and Applying the Bible* (Phillipsburg, NJ: P&R, 1996).

11. Daniel M. Doriani, *Putting the Truth to Work: The Theory and Practice of Biblical Application* (Phillipsburg, NJ: P&R, 2001). For a succinct summary of these four questions, see Dan Doriani, "Applying Scripture," The Gospel Coalition, accessed April 26, 2022, https://www.thegospelcoalition.org.

12. For an explanation of how this wholeness is central to Jesus's teaching, see Jonathan Pennington, *The Sermon on the Mount and Human Flourishing: A Theological Commentary* (Grand Rapids, MI: Baker Academic, 2018).

13. See Jason Hood, *Imitating God in Christ: Recapturing a Biblical Pattern* (Downers Grove, IL: IVP Academic, 2013), 23, 47; Thomas Watson, "The Godly Man's Picture Drawn with a Scripture Pencil," in *Discourses on Important and Interesting Subjects: Being the Select Works of Thomas Watson*, vol. 1 (Glasgow: Blackie, Fullarton, 1829), 404.

14. Doriani, "Applying Scripture."

15. Doriani, "Applying Scripture."

16. Doriani, "Applying Scripture."

17. Quoted in Erin Heim, *Adoption in Galatians and Romans: Contemporary Metaphor Theories and the Pauline Huiothesia Metaphors* (Leiden: Brill, 2017), 37.

18. The world of scholarship on metaphors and language is large. The classic starting point is George Lakoff and Mark Johnson, *Metaphors We Live By* (Chicago: Universtiy of Chicago Press, 2003).

19. Joel Green, *Seized by Truth: Reading the Bible as Scripture* (Nashville: Abingdon, 2007), 161.

20. Green, *Seized by Truth*, 11–12.

21. The images of a safari and pilgrimage are inspired by Green, *Seized by Truth*, 13, 56. The Viking one is mine.

22. Eugene Peterson, *Eat This Book: A Conversation in the Art of Spiritual Reading* (Grand Rapids, MI: Eerdmans, 2009), 6.

23. Kyle Roberts, *Emerging Prophet: Kierkegaard and the Postmodern People of God* (Eugene, OR: Cascade, 2013), 8–9.

24. Hans Boersma, *Scripture as Real Presence: Sacramental Exegesis in the Early Church* (Grand Rapids, MI: Baker Academic, 2018), 263.

25. Thomas à Kempis, *The Imitation of Christ* (Milwaukee: Bruce, 1940), bk. 1, chap. 1, https://www.ccel.org/ccel/kempis/imitation.all.html.

26. One modern introduction to this practice is Thomas Keating, *Open Mind, Open Heart* (London: Bloomsbury Continuum, 2006).

27. Catherine Bell, *Ritual Theory, Ritual Practice* (Oxford: Oxford University Press, 2009), 100, quoted in Dru Johnson, *Human Rites: The Power of Rituals, Habits, and Sacraments* (Grand Rapids, MI: Eerdmans, 2019), 17.

28. Westminster Confession of Faith 1.5. See "The Westminster Confession of Faith," Ligonier Ministries, May 12, 2021, https://www.ligonier.org.

29. J. V. Fesko, "The Self Attestation of Scripture and Internal Witness of the Holy Spirit," The Gospel Coalition, accessed April 27, 2022, https://www.thegospelcoalition.org.

30. John Owen, *The Holy Spirit* (Grand Rapids, MI: Kregel, 1954), 155.

31. Included at the end of Pius XI, *Studiorum Ducem* [Encyclical Letter on Thomas Aquinas], June 29, 1923, https://www.papalencyclicals.net.

32. John Calvin speaks of the church as a nurturing mother in his *Institutes of the Christian Religion*, ed. John T. McNeill, trans. Ford Lewis Battles, 2 vols. (Philadelphia: Westminster, 1960), 4.1.1–4 (2:1011–16). This is discussed in Kevin J. Vanhoozer, *Hearers and Doers: A Pastor's Guide to Making Disciples through Scripture and Doctrine* (Bellingham, WA: Lexham, 2019), 166–67.

Epilogue: The Final Destination

1. "Bible Verses Explained: John 1:1—'In the Beginning Was the Word,'" JW.org, accessed April 28, 2022, https://www.jw.org.

2. "Bible Verses Explained: John 1:1—'In the Beginning Was the Word.'"

3. Eugene Peterson, *Eat This Book: A Conversation in the Art of Spiritual Reading* (Grand Rapids, MI: Eerdmans, 2009), 58.

General Index

Scripture Index